A History of Women's Lives in Oxford

A History of Women's Lives in Oxford

By Nell Darby

AN IMPRINT OF PEN & SWORD BOOKS LTD.
YORKSHIRE – PHILADELPHIA

First published in Great Britain in 2019 by
Pen & Sword History
An imprint of
Pen & Sword Books Limited
Yorkshire - Philadelphia

Copyright © Nell Darby, 2019

ISBN 978 1 52671 785 6

The right of Nell Darby to be identified as Author of this work has been asserted by her in accordance with the Copyright, Designs and Patents Act 1988.

A CIP catalogue record for this book is available from the British Library

All rights reserved. No part of this book may be reproduced or transmitted in any form or by any means, electronic or mechanical including photocopying, recording or by any information storage and retrieval system, without permission from the Publisher in writing.

Typeset in 11.5/14 point Times New Roman
by Aura Technology and Software Services, India

Printed and bound in the UK
by TJ International, Padstow, Cornwall

Pen & Sword Books Limited incorporates the imprints of Atlas, Archaeology, Aviation, Discovery, Family History, Fiction, History, Maritime, Military, Military Classics, Politics, Select, Transport, True Crime, Air World, Frontline Publishing, Leo Cooper, Remember When, Seaforth Publishing, The Praetorian Press, Wharncliffe Local History, Wharncliffe Transport, Wharncliffe True Crime and White Owl.

For a complete list of Pen & Sword titles please contact
PEN & SWORD BOOKS LIMITED
47 Church Street, Barnsley, South Yorkshire S70 2AS, United Kingdom
E-mail: enquiries@pen-and-sword.co.uk
Website: www.pen-and-sword.co.uk

Or
PEN AND SWORD BOOKS
1950 Lawrence Rd, Havertown, PA 19083, USA
E-mail: Uspen-and-sword@casematepublishers.com
Website: www.penandswordbooks.com

Contents

Acknowledgements vii

Introduction viii

Chapter One   Education   1

Chapter Two   Work   16

Chapter Three   Home   29

Chapter Four   Food & Drink   40

Chapter Five   Health   52

Chapter Six   Leisure   61

Chapter Seven   Prison Life   74

Chapter Eight   Active Citizens   86

Conclusion   108

References   110

Primary Works Consulted   131

Index   136

Acknowledgements

The British Newspaper Archive is a fantastic resource for searching for local newspaper articles – enabling the researcher to find out what was happening in a location, and what was deemed of interest both to the local press and their local readers. This book has been mainly researched using the BNA, and I would like to thank those who have made it such a good and easy-to-use resource. Thanks are also due to those who compile and write Oxford's local history websites that have enabled me to double-check some facts – in particular, Stephanie Jenkins for her fascinating and detailed Headington and Oxford History websites (www.headington.org.uk and www.oxfordhistory.org.uk). For anyone interested in the city's history, I'd recommend a read of these. I would also like to thank the staff of the Bodleian Libraries, and in particular, those at the Weston Library and Law Library, who have been consistently helpful. Thanks are due, too, to Oliver Mahony, the archivist at St Hilda's College, and to Andrew Chapman.

Thanks also to my own Oxford ancestors – the members of the Harper family who lived and worked in the city in the nineteenth century, from Pembroke Street to Park Town. The male members of the family worked here as accountants, dentists, wine merchants, photographers and university librarians. Their ghosts have been with me during the writing of the book – but so too have the ghosts of their wives and daughters, whose lives and roles are less documented, a perennial issue. Knowing the strong women in my family today, though, I have no doubt that they would have been actively involved in their male relatives' work lives as well as their personal lives.

Finally, as always, thanks to John, Jake and Eva Darby – and also to Rosie Farr, for both running and writing support.

Introduction

The period from 1850 to 1950 was a time of great change, not just in Oxford, but across the country. Britain changed from being a rural nation to an increasingly urban one, as industrialisation had a huge impact both on the size of towns and cities, and on what jobs were available within them. More housing was needed to accommodate those moving into these urban areas for work, and so the towns spread, and suburbs appeared to house both new workers, and those seeking to move out of polluted centres.

Oxford was different to some places; although it was a 'small provincial city with no industrial base', it had plenty of job opportunities, and so, throughout the Victorian period, it grew 'steadily'.[1] Yet, despite the continuing interest about life in Victorian Britain, in the 1980s it was noted that far more was known about Oxford during the medieval era than during the Victorian era, a fascinating time for the city as it grew and developed. In fact, in the sixty years between 1841 and 1901, the censuses show that Oxford's population more than doubled.[2] Many came from rural areas in search of work, but they were also attracted by the city's amenities and attractions, which offered a social life that individuals did not have in their rural villages.[3] Transport in and out of the city also encouraged visitors and migrants, and transport routes improved over the second half of the nineteenth century. In June 1844, the Great Western Railway started routes to Oxford – although initially, the terminus was at Grandpont in south Oxford, with a new city centre station at Park End Street opening in 1852.[4] There was a clear differentiation between town and gown, as there had been for centuries; yet both were seeing change throughout this time, from the improvements in transportation and health care, to the opening up of university education to women.

The relative absence of comprehensive histories of Oxford and its people is clear from a search of local bookshops and tourist sites in the city. There is a domination of books aimed at the tourist – introductions to the city that focus on its beauty and its architecture, but where are the books that look at life behind the spires and, more specifically, the lives of the city's female residents? The lives of poorer women, in particular, can be marginalised in history books just as women's lives themselves have been marginalised throughout history; yet their experiences could often be different from men's, being proscribed by them, and influenced by their male relatives' status. How did men's lives impact on women's in Oxford – and how did women react, or spend their time? How did they seek to improve the city, and the lives of its residents, or improve their own education and work? These are some of the questions considered when planning this book.

The book does not, though, set out to offer a comprehensive history of Oxford in the century from 1850, or of its university, its best-known asset. It would be both impossible to do so, and there are other books and websites out there that can offer insights into aspects of these histories. Neither can I cover all of Oxford's women and their individual experiences. The experience of my Oxford ancestors – from the wife of one of the city's pioneer photographers, to her daughter, dead from consumption in her early twenties, before she had a chance to fully bloom – are not representative of many others, for example. What I do hope to do is to offer a snapshot of changing lives and times, and of the contribution women made to the city.

This is an individualistic selection of stories and activities, drawn from both archives and newspapers. The latter offer a gendered insight into women's lives, often being accounts written by men (although some reports of events may have been submitted to the local press by the city's women). Likewise, census entries up to 1911 were compiled largely by men (although there were some female census enumerators), and in 1911, the census forms were filled in by the head of household which, in many cases, might be the husband or father of a family, so again present a gendered history; how a man might describe his wife's or daughter's occupation might not reflect how she would have written it herself, for example, although one hopes that her family would recognise her position and record it accurately. Where the 1911 census is particularly fascinating is in its entries concerning supporters of the suffragist movement, where women might refuse to fill in their details, or only record the basics – here we get a picture of women seeking control and political power, expressing their beliefs and their strength through the collation of the national census.

There is also, perhaps inevitably given the sources I have chosen, a class bias. Press reports of local women's achievements tended to focus on the middle and upper classes – the wives or daughters of vicars, lawyers, and Oxford academics, who were often to be found organising teas, supporting the male members of their families in political or social events, or, as time progressed, becoming members of societies and movements, or becoming part of the university's student or staff population. Those from further down the social ladder had their lives recorded less frequently (although this started to change in the early twentieth century, and certainly by the 1920s). In the nineteenth century, many references to working-class girls and women relate to their criminal exploits – trials increasingly providing quick and cheap copy for newspapers. I've chosen to include these as a separate chapter, because of the usefulness such reports have in giving us a picture of the difficulties of life for poorer or less educated individuals, struggling to get by while wealthier families thrived. But there is inevitably some overlap between topics and subjects; the issue of child mortality, for example, belongs both in health and in home, for although illness and death is part of health and the improvements made in both environment and healthcare, the death of an individual also has a huge impact on the home life of that person's family. Feeling that someone is missing affects how you live your life and for women at home, the death of their husband could also have a huge financial impact on them, and this book shows how it could send them to the workhouse – or even their own deaths – in a short space of time.

However, what the book ultimately shows is that there was not a universal female experience in Oxford even within a relatively tight timescale; women lived individual lives, reacted differently to situations, wanted different things from life. From the pioneer female students at the university, to the 16-year-old wife who decided to become a professional singer rather than stay with her middle-aged husband, Oxford has a long history of independent or conventional women – and this book recognises, and celebrates, them.

CHAPTER ONE

Education

It is impossible to write about the women of Oxford without looking at education – how did women fit into the rigid formality and patriarchal set-up of the university, and what were the options open to intelligent, academically minded young women in the Victorian city? In the mid-nineteenth century, girls could get an education, but it was not until the 1870 Elementary Education Act that such an education became set down in legislation. This act aimed to provide a universal education, although hostility among some quarters was evident, with there being a fear that it would give the labouring classes ideas above their station. The Act set out to establish school boards that would provide an education to children between the ages of 5 and 13. Parents had to pay for this schooling – unless they were poor, in which case the school boards would pay. In the decade following the passing of the Elementary Education Act, between 3,000 and 4,000 schools were either started or transferred to school board control across England and Wales.[1] However, even after the passing of the Act, schooling was not compulsory; it was only with the passing of another Elementary Education Act in 1880 – one of eight more passed between 1873 and 1883 – that schooling was made compulsory to the age of 10. In 1891, elementary education became free for all. In 1902, the school boards were replaced by local education authorities.

By the end of the nineteenth century, plenty of schools existed for girls to get an education, from small board schools to private schools – and the role of the governess still gave well-to-do girls an education even when their parents were reluctant to send them to a school. Females did not just benefit from being able to attend school – they were also able to become schoolmistresses themselves. Elizabeth Alden was one, running a school on the Banbury Road as a 64-year-old in 1881, helped by her daughters; 28-year-old Annie Alden, for example, was responsible for teaching the girls music and drawing. It was not unusual for widowed women to take on the running of their own schools, assisted by their single daughters, or for spinsters to operate schools with their unmarried sisters. In the latter case, Caroline Cook ran a school at Paradise Square, in the parish of St Ebbe's, with her sister Emily as housekeeper, another sister, Matilda, as assistant teacher, and two teenage nieces, Florence and Charlotte, as music teachers. However, until the passing of the Sex Disqualification Removal Act in 1919, teachers had to be widowed or single; married women were not allowed to teach formally, and a woman, on getting married, would need to resign.[2]

A key development in the education of Oxford girls occurred in 1875, when the Oxford High School for Girls was founded by the Girls' Day School Trust; today, the school – Oxford's oldest girls' school – remembers its history as over '140 years of pioneering women and innovative girls' education'.[3] It opened on 3 November at the Judges' Lodgings – St Giles' House, at 16 St Giles – and initially had twenty-nine students and three teachers, under the headmistress, Ada Benson.

Ada was part of a well-known family herself. She was born on 27 November 1840 at Winson Green, now part of inner-city Birmingham, the daughter of Edward White Benson and his wife Harriet. At the time of her baptism, on 24 December 1840 at St Martin's in Birmingham, Edward was listed as being a chemist. She was part of a large family, with brothers Edward White and Christopher, and sisters Harriet, Eleanor and Emmeline; her eldest brother Edward started his career as a schoolmaster – but later became the Archbishop of Canterbury; his fifth son, Edward Frederic, became a well-known writer, the author of the *Mapp & Lucia* society novels. The older Edward White Benson, Ada's father, died when she was just 2½. Ada's initial experience of teaching was through her older sister, Eleanor. In 1871, Eleanor, then aged 38 (eight years Ada's senior), was a school mistress at Sydney Lodge, a school in Kingston, Surrey. Ada lived with her and presumably helped out at the school, along with a Russian governess. This girls' school was small, with just eight boarders aged between 15 and 17.

Ada was 35 when she took on the challenging role of becoming the first headmistress of Oxford's first high school for girls. The local papers throughout 1875 eagerly anticipated its opening; in February that year, the *Reading Mercury* had recorded a meeting held at the town hall to discuss establishing the school. Needless to say, the chair – and most of the others on the platform to speak – were men, which was not unexpected, as many represented the university and its colleges. The 'large attendance of ladies and gentlemen' was noted, and that many of the attendees were influential members of the university. Resolutions to progress with the school were made at the meeting – and from here on in, it was full speed ahead to get the school open as soon as possible.[4]

However, the school had been due to open on 18 October 1875, with adverts being placed in the *Oxford Journal* from the previous month. For example, on 25 September, an advertisement stated:

> Oxford High School for Girls. Headmistress Miss Benson. The Council of the Girls' Public Day School Company (Limited) give Notice that the above School will OPEN on Monday October 18th next, at 16 St Giles's Street. A Preliminary Prospectus has been issued, which, with the requisite forms for admission, can be obtained at M.A. Matthews's, 66 St Giles Street, Oxford, or from the Secretary of the Company, 112 Brompton Road, London SW.[5]

But then, on 9 October – just a week before its intended opening – a further advert stated:

> Oxford High School for Girls. The Council of the Girls' Public Day School Company (Limited) regret to announce that, owing to

unexpected legal difficulties, the above School will NOT open as previously advertised. Offices of the Company, 112 Brompton Road, London SW.[6]

The school duly opened in November, with a preparatory department educating girls aged between 4 and 7 opening in January 1877.[7] At the start of 1879, the school relocated to 38 St Giles', then 21 Banbury Road in 1881, where it stayed until moving to its current location on Belbroughton Road in 1957.[8] In 1879, however, Ada Benson resigned as headmistress due to illness; later the same year, she married company secretary Andrew McDowall, but died three years later, on 11 October 1882, at Bedford, aged just short of 42 years old.

She was replaced by Matilda Ellen Bishop, the school's second head, who was then aged 32. Unlike her girls, she lived on site at St Giles, together with two female housekeepers. In 1891, Matilda was listed as the principal of Royal Holloway College in London, and by 1911 she would be the principal of the St Gabriel's Training College in Camberwell; Matilda died there on 1 July 1913. Her career shows that the growing education sector would increasingly provide opportunities for single women to gain a productive, rewarding and challenging career ensuring that a new generation of women could be educated – and educated well.

Oxford's girls could go to school; but what about university? These had always been male bastions of education, but in the late nineteenth century, calls grew for women to be admitted. However, as Pauline Adams has put it, Oxford University was 'a late convert to the idea of educating women'.[9] The 1870s, however, saw the start of the long process of enabling women to get a university education in Oxford. There had been considerable resistance in the city to female education at this level, but in 1867, the decade-old Oxford Delegacy of Local Examinations let schoolgirls enter its examinations, and in 1875, it was enabled to run examinations for women over the age of 18, 'of a standard roughly equivalent to university finals'.[10]

In 1866, 44-year-old Eleanor Smith – herself the sister of Henry Smith, Savillian Professor of Geometry, and later fellow of Corpus

Christi – had established a series of lectures for women, with lecturers including Mark Pattison, the Rector of Lincoln College (1813–1884), Henry Nettleship (1839–1893) and Merton College's William Sidgwick.[11] The scheme didn't last long, simply because there were relatively few women in Oxford who were able to take part.[12] At this time, only men without wives were able to be fellows of the Oxford colleges, but once married men were allowed – from 1871 – the city became home with many more young, intelligent married women who not only wanted to educate themselves, but their daughters too.

From this point on, lectures for women became a more feasible long-term prospect, and the establishment of a female college or hall became a focus of supporters of female education in the city. In 1878, a meeting was held, chaired by the master of University College, to discuss whether Oxford, like other cities, needed an Association for Promoting the Higher Education of Women (AEW).[13] This association would provide teaching for women over the age of 19, on condition that they had suitable accommodation. Out of this need for residences, the Society of Home-Students was created in 1879 by two men: Henry Nettleship, who had lectured for Eleanor Smith in the 1860s, and the political radical Thomas Hill Green (1836–1882). Green was chair of its committee for ten years, as well as being vice-president of the Council of Somerville College to cater for those on AEW courses who lodged with private families in the city (a cheaper way of studying at the university); out of this society emerged St Anne's College.[14] The Society of Home-Students was a radical invention, with the laudable goal of making it possible for any student, from any background, to study at Oxford if they had the ability and determination.[15]

In the same year as the creation of the Society of Home-Students came the opening of two women-only colleges at Oxford – Lady Margaret Hall and Somerville, the latter named for astronomer, geographer and mathematician Mary Somerville (1780–1872). Eleanor Smith, who had pioneered university-style lectures for women nearly twenty years earlier, helped to found the college and was one of its original council members. She continued to campaign for Oxford degrees to be issued to women.[16] The first day of the first term at Somerville was Monday, 13 October 1879, with students whose ages spanned from 17 to 36.[17]

In 1886, St Hugh's College opened, followed seven years later by St Hilda's College.[18] St Hilda's was founded by the principal of Cheltenham Ladies' College, Dorothea Beale (1831–1906) specifically so that students from her school could progress to attending lectures at Oxford.[19] Its first principal was a middle-aged widow from Chipping Norton, the market town some twenty miles north of Oxford. This was Esther Burrows, the daughter of Chipping Norton's most well-known resident, William Bliss, a woollen manufacturer whose mill is still the key focal point of the town today. She had married brewer Henry Parker Burrows on 8 September 1870 in her home town, an event that garnered extensive press coverage in the *Oxford Times* and elsewhere. Esther had married in white satin, with six bridesmaids and two little flower-girls, and the wedding led to the church bells being rung throughout the day. Aged 23 at the time, she must have thought her future was assured; her husband was a well-established Berkshire man, sociable, but of 'particularly abstemious habits' – they would have children, and she would live the life typical of a wealthy industrialist's married daughter.[20]

But fate had other ideas. While five months' pregnant with their first (and only) child, Esther was suddenly widowed. Her husband had been dining with some old friends at Maidenhead Thicket in Berkshire one evening in October 1871. He had just poured himself a glass of sherry, and as he went to put the decanter down on the table, a blood vessel ruptured at the base of his brain and he died instantly. The premature and sudden death – Henry was just 38 – shocked both his friends and family, and left Esther both an expectant mother and a widow. Her husband's effects were valued at between £14,000 and £16,000 – roughly between £640,000 and £730,000 today – so she was financially comfortable, and even in the 1881 census, she was listed as living off 'income from investment'. However, widowhood and financial security also enabled her, eventually, to seek a career. In 1891, she was running a boarding-house for female students in

Cheltenham, where her daughter Christine Mary Elizabeth also appears to have been studying.

By the time of the 1901 census, Esther was well-established in her new career as principal of 'St Hilda's Hall' in Oxford, with daughter Christine, now 29, acting as vice-principal. When Esther retired in 1910, her daughter took over as principal of St Hilda's, a post she held until 1919. She would then become principal of the Society of Home-Students from 1921 to 1929.[21] Esther died on 20 February 1935 at her home at 47 Woodstock Road. Daughter Christine, who never married, died at her Oxford care home in 1959, aged 87, and was buried at St Giles on 14 September that year.

Who were the first women to matriculate at Oxford's female colleges? Luckily, a photograph of the first class of Lady Margaret Hall students, from 1879, survives, with the names of the nine women inscribed at the bottom.[22] They were Mary Smith, Charlotte Ward, Louisa Digges La Touche, Eliza Dorothy Bradby, Laura Jones, Edith Pearson, Evelyn Anstruther, Edith Ayles and Winifred Cobbe. Eliza Dorothy Bradby, one of those listed, was from Harrow, born in the autumn of 1861, but brought up in Hertfordshire and London. Her father, Edward Henry Bradby (d.1893), was a clergyman born in Calcutta, India, the nephew of a Royal Navy commander and himself educated at Oxford; her mother Ellen was from the Isle of Wight. This was an educated, fairly wealthy family. Edward was not only a clergyman, but also master of Haileybury College in Hertfordshire, where he and his family were from at least 1869 to 1881. In the 1881 census, Eliza, then aged 19, is described as a 'student', as are her younger siblings. She was the eldest of seven children, having younger siblings Godfrey, Mabel, Edward, Henry, Mary, and Lucy. Eliza's brother, Edward, was an articled clerk in a solicitor's office in 1891, and by 1911 was a solicitors' manager; her other brothers, Godfrey and Christopher, were tutors and schoolmasters.

Eliza Dorothy Bradby never married. In 1911, aged 49, she was still living at home with her widowed mother and siblings Edward and Mary. They were wealthy enough to have five servants and live in Bayswater. She died in Warwickshire in 1927, her effects being worth the considerable £14,879. This was the typical female Oxford student; usually from a professional, middle-class family, where the male siblings had received a good level of education, and where the parents may have travelled or otherwise received a wider worldview than others less fortunate. Many of the students aspired to teaching as a career after their studies finished – if they needed a career at all. As Pauline Adams has stated, out of the 155 students who started their studies at Somerville between 1879 and 1890, fifty-nine went onto become teachers, and fifty-one married.[23] Indeed, the opening up of university-level examinations to women (albeit without the attainment of a degree) had been primarily a response to the need to produce well-qualified teachers at schools across the country.[24]

In 1883, *The Guardian* reported that the AEW had been so successful in establishing Lady Margaret and Somerville, and in providing 'a regular course of instruction organised with reference to the university examinations for women', that it had been encouraged to provide a correspondence, or distance-learning, course, which would meet the requirements of the university examinations, but would be open to any woman who wanted to learn this way. The teachers appointed by the AEW would be either university graduates or women who had themselves passed the higher examinations. The courses would last for four terms, each of eight weeks, and cost a guinea a term for pass level subjects, or twenty-five shillings a term for Honour subjects. This course was designed explicitly to 'many young women who either cannot be spared from home duties, or cannot afford to come and live at one of the halls, or whose friends dislike the notion of 'ladies' colleges' and hold that girls who want to study must do the best for themselves at home.' It was recognised that many girls struggled to learn on their own from home, yet were keen for 'mental improvement' and simply needed a bit of supervision.[25] Yet the AEW clearly recognised here the fight against ingrained prejudice towards women's education; the concern that in studying, a woman would not be undertaking her domestic responsibilities, and that that should be her primary occupation. The fact that women were increasingly vocalising their desire for more, for the opportunities that had for so long been open to men, was clear: the AEW clearly thought there was a need for more education, rather than less, and recognised the value of providing education in both traditional and non-traditional contexts. But initially, women were very much outsiders in the university world. They were frequently chaperoned in lectures, 'to make sure they made no unsuitable friendships or were approached by men'.[26]

There were undoubtedly many academically able women in the city who were keen to benefit from the education that was available to men. They could go to lectures, take exams, and get grades for those exams – but they were not allowed to matriculate; unlike men, they could not get a degree in return for their hard work. This was such with one case, involving the daughter of a key Oxford figure. On 13 June 1893, at the Headmaster's House attached to Christ Church Cathedral School, a little baby girl was born. She was named Dorothy Leigh Sayers, and she would grow up to become a well-known and respected crime writer. Her father, Reverend Henry Sayers, was a chaplain of Christ Church, and head of the choir school, and so Dorothy began her life in this salubrious Oxford setting – her birth there now being marked by a blue plaque. She was baptised at Christ Church on 15 July 1893, by her father. Although Sayers herself was not brought up in Oxford, she returned to the city of her birth in 1912, when she won a scholarship to study modern languages and medieval literature at Somerville College. Sayers ended her studies with first-class honours three years later, but because women could not be awarded degrees she had to wait until the law was changed in the autumn of 1920 to receive her MA.

Dorothy, of course, was by no means alone. Annie Mary Anne Henley Rogers, for example, has the distinction of having become the first woman to gain honours in an Oxford university examination. She had originally sat the Local Examinations in 1873, entering under her initials, which did not expose her gender. She performed so well that she won an exhibition (scholarship) to Worcester College – only for it to then be discovered that she was a woman, and the exhibition rapidly withdrawn.[27] In 1877, she was given first class honours in Latin and Greek after sitting as part of the 'examinations for women'. Two years later, she gained first-class honours in ancient history – but it wasn't until 26 October 1920 that she was allowed to both matriculate and graduate. Annie was 21 when she gained her first honours, but 64 when she graduated.

Annie was a native of Oxford and daughter of James Edwin Thorold Rogers and his wife, Ann Susannah Charlotte, née Reynolds. She was born at Wellington Place on 15 February 1856 and baptised at St Giles on 2 April 1856. Her father – known as Thorold – was an educated man, being curate of Headington and a professor of political economy. He too had been a student at Oxford, graduating from Magdalen College in 1849; in 1880 he stood down from being a clergyman in order to stand for parliament – he was the Liberal MP for Southwark until 1886.[28] His daughter was therefore brought up in a literate, politically aware, social family with a knowledge of life outside Oxford (her father was originally from Hampshire, and her mother from Marylebone).

Perhaps significantly, she was the eldest child but only daughter, and her four brothers' education may have stressed to her how unfair the status quo was with regard to the education of women. Not only was Annie the first woman to gain an education at Oxford university, she was also the first female don – the 1901 census records her as a tutor and lecturer, and the 1911 census as a tutor to the university's women students. In 1936, she was made an honorary fellow of St Hugh's College. She never married; after her parents' deaths (James died in 1890, aged 67, and Ann in 1899, aged 73) she lived on her own or with a brother, maintaining a career that a generation earlier would not have been possible. Annie died in 1937 at the age of 81, in the city where she had been born and bred.

Annie's achievement in 1879 was such that she had been recorded at the head of the list of Oxford Local Examinations for women in the local press, just ahead of Mabel Charlotte Bradley, who had passed her preliminary examinations.[29] Mabel, originally from Marlborough in Wiltshire, had been living in Oxford since 1870; her father, George Granville Bradley, had been the master of Marlborough College before moving to Oxford to be head of

University College, where he had himself studied, gaining both an MA and Doctorate in Divinity.[30] Mabel herself, after passing her prelims, moved onto Kensington High School for Girls. Her educated family, and her own success academically, led to a career of her own as a novelist and critic. She died in Earl's Court in July 1936, by which time her businessman husband, John Henry Birchenough, had been knighted.

The fight to be awarded degrees was a long one. In March 1896, the Oxford University Congregation had 'again' declared against women being allowed to gain degrees, but it was noted by the press at this time that the tide was turning. For months, the question of granting a BA to women had been debated by both Oxford and Cambridge; one newspaper noted that although,

> the forces of sheer conservatism have again triumphed ... the battle will be renewed and the ultimate issue can scarcely be regarded as doubtful. It is indeed remarkable that at Oxford and Cambridge, the two highest seats of learning in the kingdom, the title of women to graduation should still be disputed; whereas the eight other universities and eleven university colleges no longer make sex a disqualification.[31]

So in this sense, Oxford was seen as backward and old-fashioned; it was noted that it was absurd that for nearly two decades, women had been allowed to attend the same lectures and get the same teaching as men, that they had been allowed to take the same exams – but when they passed – even if with better marks than men – they were not allowed a degree or to graduate. The prejudice that had attached to women studying at Oxford – that it would 'degrade' them, and 'soften' men – was recognised as being unenlightened, and so the Oxford vote (which was 213 against versus 140 for) was not seen as the end.[32]

However, some other restrictions on women students also existed. Perhaps the most bizarre, to our modern eyes, was the concept of chaperoning. From the earliest days of women being permitted to attend lectures that were also attended by men, a female chaperone had to come with them, and sit through the lectures, to ensure that lone women would have some protection from the male students. Often, this would be a member of staff from one of the women's halls; it could mean that these women had to sit through lectures whose subjects they were entirely disinterested in – with one even resorting to knitting her way through lectures. This system of chaperoning – baulked at by many female students – was only abolished in 1925.[33] In other cases, there were rules preventing women from walking arm-in-arm with male friends in public, let alone entering a male friend's rooms (either within or without a college), and rules governing what female students should wear.[34]

Of course, during the period that Oxford's female students had been able to study, but not to gain a degree, the First World War had broken out. During the period of the war, women had continued to study – with the AEW, for example, putting on a series of lectures on war-related themes.[35] In fact, women now formed the bulk of Oxford's students, as many male students and dons were enlisted for active service. Teaching staff therefore had to be drawn from female as well as male ranks, and female students occupied the war-quietened buildings. This is not to say that the women's lives at university continued as before; Somerville's buildings were requisitioned by the War Office as a military hospital, necessitating the Somerville students' relocation to Oriel – a male college, but one that was currently largely empty because of the exodus of male undergraduates to the fields of war.[36]

The suffragist movement also gathered pace in the early years of the century, and in the aftermath of the armistice, the parliamentary franchise was extended to women aged 30 and over, a recognition that women had 'proved themselves' (as if that were needed!) while men were away fighting. It was anomalous that women could vote – and this applied to the female students of sufficient age to apply to be electors for the university's own parliamentary constituency – but could not gain a degree from the same university. It is therefore not surprising that another consequence, perhaps, of the First World War is that it speeded up the movement towards gaining women the degrees they had been working for over the prior decades. In 1919, the Sex Disqualification (Removal) Act enabled Oxford to matriculate women without requiring a separate Act of Parliament, and so a statute was drawn up that year, and passed, enabling women to matriculate. It was only in the October of 1920 that this statute came into effect, allowing women to be admitted as full members of the university and to graduate. The statute permitted women who had already finished their studies to gain the degree they would normally have got had they been men.[37] This meant that at the first formal graduation ceremony that women scholars could attend, some fifty-two women graduated.[38]

There was not universal acceptance of this move towards women's equality at the university, with, in 1926, there being a debate in the Oxford Union proposing that the women's colleges should be 'razed to the ground'. But even this was ground-breaking in its own way, as Somerville College's Lucy Sutherland was invited to speak at the debate – being the first female undergraduate to be invited to do so. Unfortunately, however, the motion was carried, and although it was regarded as a less than serious event, shortly afterwards, the university council was petitioned by the Hebdomadal Council (the university's executive body, 'hebdomadal' simply meaning 'weekly') to restrict the number of women students allowed at the university – and this petition was approved. A quota for each of the women's colleges was imposed, and a ban placed on new female colleges being established, if their creation would result in there being fewer than four male students to every female.[39]

Just four years after the decision to place quotas on the number of female students – which resulted in Somerville only being allowed 150 students, out of a total of 840 women students at Oxford – Helen Darbishire became the principal of the college, replacing the retiring Margery Fry. Helen had a long association with the university and the college, having started tutoring at Somerville nearly a quarter of a century earlier.[40] She was an Oxford girl, having been born in the city in 1881. This isn't to say that she wasn't well travelled, however; although Pauline Adams has stated that 'at the age of 50, [she] had spent only four years of her life outside Oxford, three as a lecturer at the Royal Holloway College and one in America as visiting professor at Wellesley', records show that she did venture outside of the city, and at an earlier age, more often than this statement suggests.[41] The 1911 census records her as visiting her family in Sidmouth, Devon, for example.

She was the daughter of Manchester-born Florence Eckersley and Londoner Samuel Dukinfield Darbishire. At the time of her birth, Helen's father had been a physician based at 15 New Inn Hall Street in Oxford; he died in 1892, aged 46, when Helen was still just 10 years old. But the family had not been in Oxford for the duration, and it isn't correct to say that Helen grew up in the city. By 1891, the Darbishire family, including 10-year-old Helen, were living in Dwygyfylchi in Caernarvonshire, Wales, and Samuel had retired. In fact, although the Dukinfields were from the north-west of England – Samuel's father, also Samuel, was a magistrate from Rotherham, and his mother Mary was from Manchester – they had settled in Caernarvonshire by 1861, and so the younger Samuel had simply returned, with his family, to the area he was brought up in once he retired. He died in Wales, too, leaving effects valued at over £10,000.

This background shows that Helen was typical of many of Oxford's female students in the late nineteenth and early twentieth centuries. She was from an affluent, educated family; although she was born and raised in Oxford, none of her family were from the city and they travelled around the country during their lives for work or family reasons. Her grandparents had employed a raft of servants, as well as a governess, and this would have been perfectly normal for many of the future Oxford students growing up. Unlike many of her fellow students, however, Helen did not marry after finishing her studies, or become a schoolteacher. Instead, she became a tutor and lecturer at the university. In 1925, then living at Radcliffe House on Woodstock Road, and aged 44, she travelled firstly to Liverpool, where she then set sail across the Atlantic for Boston.[42] Presumably this was her journey towards Wellesley, and her year as a visiting professor there.

Helen Darbishire remained principal until 1945, seeing her college through another world war. During this time, her college agreed to give more financial help to refugee students, to oversee a visit from the Town Clerk, who wanted to turn the college into a first aid centre in case there were any air raids.[43] She retired to Shepherds How, Grasmere, in the Lake District, where she died on 11 March 1961. Her obituary, in the *Illustrated London News*, she was described as 'one of the world's leading authorities on William Wordsworth and the Lake poets', and so her last home was just as appropriate for this scholar as her previous one in the city of dreaming spires.[44]

CHAPTER TWO

Work

Women worked in various trades in Oxford, although during the nineteenth and early twentieth centuries, they were limited somewhat by their gender. It was acceptable for women to take on jobs as governesses, as milliners and dressmakers, as servants and, from the 1860s onwards, as shopgirls.

Milliners were often, although not always, women (in the eighteenth and early nineteenth centuries, men who became milliners were perceived as rather feminine, and portrayed in the papers as a bit 'wet' and worthy of mockery). Catherine Woods, an 18-year-old painter's daughter, was working as a milliner in 1881 (as were her next door neighbours, Gertrude and Emily Mason); 30 years later, 25-year-old Daisy Walter, daughter of a physics professor's assistant, was doing the same job. Dressmakers were similarly usually women – at the lower level, this was a job that could be done from home, alongside childcare responsibilities, although some women set up in business either on their own or with other women, advertising their services in the press. Notices of dissolutions of partnerships in the local papers shows that this could be a precarious act, with some personal relationships breaking down alongside business failures. They might specialise in a particular item – for example, one 1903 advert asked for 'a good tailoress, also one experienced in Ladies' Coats', to apply to 21 Walton Street for a job.[1]

In 1871, dressmakers working from home vied for space with the shops on the High; Mary Payne, 35, described herself as a 'former dressmaker' at number 11, while her daughter Helen, 16, was following her mother's trade. At number 25, both Mary Harvey, 29, and her 21-year-old sister Alice were working as dressmakers – however, their other two sisters, Laura and Kate, did not have an occupation. Although the sewing machine had been invented back in the eighteenth century, with various improvements and new designs being patented throughout the first half of the nineteenth century, it was in the middle of the century that the machine began to really revolutionise the dressmaking industry. The American inventor Isaac Merritt Singer patented his own sewing machine in 1851; in England, William Jones and Thomas Chadwick, working as Chadwick & Jones, produced sewing machines from their factory in Ashton-under-Lyne, Lancashire, from 1860 until 1863, before continuing production separately. Dressmakers and clothing manufacturers, could now, if they could afford them, purchase machines to produce ready-to-wear clothes. Electric machines were available from 1889, and by the end of the First World War, consumers and manufacturers alike could choose from hand, treadle or electric machines. In 1903, one advert in the *Oxford Times* was advertising for:

> RESPECTABLE GIRLS, from the age of 16 and upwards, wishing to learn the SEWING MACHINE should apply to W.F. Lucas and Co, 59 George Street, Oxford. Good money earned after one month's teaching. For terms, apply personally any day except Saturday.[2]

The Industrial Revolution had led to an increase in consumerism and consumption and over the course of the nineteenth century, migration from the countryside to towns and cities such as Oxford meant that there were more residents needing to buy more things.[3] In addition, improving forms of transportation meant a wider range of goods could be imported and sold. Whereas traditionally, shops had employed boys to sell their goods, in the 1860s, they began to employ girls. Pamela Cox and Annabel Hobley have noted that the main reason for this was cost – women's salaries were lower than men, and so by employing female staff, shop owners could reduce their costs and increase profits.⁴ Also, though, because of this increasing demand for goods, the number of shops in Britain was increasing – and a larger number of shops meant a need for more staff. Girls were increasingly employed in all types of shop, from the smallest to the large drapery or, later, department stores, with adverts for shopgirls stressing the need for respectable girls – this was promoted as a good job for those from decent backgrounds.

Located on the High Street, the City Drapery Stores was one of Oxford's popular nineteenth-century shops. Originally opened by Edward Beaumont in 1884, Charles Webber had bought the store in 1905 and gradually expanded the business by taking over several other neighbouring shops on the street. The business was bought by Hide & Co in 1952, but continued to operate until the 1970s.⁵ Another successful business was F. Cape & Co, which was started by Methodist Faithful Cape in the 1860s on St Ebbes Street, but later opened branches at 12 Little Clarendon Street, Cowley Road and Church Street, as well as maintaining its enlarged premises at 28-32 St Ebbes Street.⁶ Cape's started as a drapery – and was listed as such in the 1881 census, when the only women listed as working for him were his housekeeper, Rachel Blandy, and drapery 'shopwoman' Charlotte Simpkins – but later sold 'everything from ladies' corsets and children's hats to hosiery, haberdashery, lace, baby linen, sheeting, blankets, quilts, shoes and furnishings'. Faithful Cape and his successor, Henry Lewis, were paternalistic employers, treating their shopgirls (and men) as though they were part of a large, albeit strict, family. There was a hierarchy of staff, each level looking after the one below, and staff lived-in in quarters above the St Ebbes shop, sleeping in shared bedrooms, and also sharing a day room and dining room. There was little escape from surveillance, with their behaviour and morals monitored by their colleagues and a housekeeper.⁷ William Biggs' linen drapery and china dealer's shop was a smaller concern than Cape's. Based at 9 and 10 High Street, in 1871, Biggs was employing two male and two female draper's assistants. The female assistants were aged 21 and 26, slightly older than the age of the male employees (18 and 20).

As with other occupations opening themselves up to females, concern arose in some quarters that these shopgirls might be immoral, selling their bodies as much as the products of their shops. They were the target of male fantasies, or acerbic newspaper comments about their morals and lifestyles. Homes for shopgirls were established, where they could be looked after out-of-hours in a 'family' environment – shorthand for control – in that the girls' comings and goings could be monitored and restricted, under the excuse that they needed protecting and looking after, as can be seen from the lodgings provided by the Methodist owners of F. Cape & Co. However, in other shops, female employees might have 'protection' afforded by their own father or husband, for in these, a wife or daughters might assist the patriarch of the family in his own shop, although they were not always recognised for their roles in censuses or elsewhere, as their work was unpaid, and seen as 'helping out' rather than having a 'job'. On occasion, the women might even take over the man's business – for example, Samuel Evans was a draper based at 12 High Street in Oxford. In the 1850s and 1860s he was living and working here, with eight draper's assistants; by 1871 he had died, and his widow Jane and their daughter were running the business, still overseeing the eight assistants.

Shopgirls were not just associated with draperies and clothes shops; they were listed in a variety of shops and businesses. In 1871, for example, the census records Sarah Churchill, aged 22, as a 'shop woman' working at Joseph King's bakery on the High. These Oxford shopgirls generally earned a small wage, but were expected to look smart and respectable, and to stand for hours, smiling and selling. There were no regulated shop hours – most shop-owners would keep the shop open as long as they thought they might get business. They were also reluctant to close if another local shop was still open. There were no formal lunch hours or break times; if a customer needed serving, a girl was expected to leave her lunch and return to serve. She was also expected to sell, sell, sell – not just what the customer wanted, but also items that she had not come in for and had not previously thought she needed. It was, in short, a demanding and thankless job, despite its depiction as a rewarding occupation for the modern girl. Those living-in were also expected to be able to work as many hours as their employer deemed necessary.

There was soon disquiet about conditions, not just for shopgirls but for their male equivalents too. In the late nineteenth century, unions were formed, fighting for a reduction in working hours and proper meal breaks, and in the early twentieth century, it became compulsory to have a half-day closing one day a week. By Edwardian times, workers were asking for more rights, and gradually, shopkeepers realised that by investing in their staff, they would improve their performance – and thereby increase their own profits.[8] As part of this desire to increase their staff's motivation and commitment to their stores, some employers developed activities akin to our modern team-building – for example, Cape & Co set up a sports club for its staff, and took them on day trips. It also held an annual stocktaking party at the Cadena Café, where staff could let their hair down with games and dances – in the company of the managers.[9]

All changed with the outbreak of the First World War. Male shop staff and other workers left the city in their hundreds to fight, and women were needed to take up their roles. Therefore, women were promoted or given roles that had previously gone to men, or could leave and get jobs in other industries. Despite the horrors of war, this was a boom-time for female employment and empowerment. People had to carry on with everyday life at home, and this meant that shopping continued. There was therefore a continued need for shop staff. However, once the war ended, there was a depression with wages falling, and men returning from war to take on their own jobs. Unemployment increased, and women now faced an uncertain period – as did shop owners. The answer lay in a change both in shops and in shopping habits, making shop layouts easier for customers to browse in rather than having to ask the shopgirls for items behind the counter.[10]

In the 1930s, Cox and Hobley note that Marks & Spencer had introduced restrooms, subsidised canteens and proper training for its shopgirls.[11] When the Second World War broke out however, the stores took on another function. On 26 May 1942, the Oxford branch became home to a recruiting stand, managed by Miss Barbara Coates, NAAFI recruiting officer, and her assistant Miss Eleanor Burke. The women, who had both entered the NAAFI – the Army's canteen service – as canteen girls, were part of a campaign to encourage girls to train as NAAFI assistants, and Oxford had been set the target of signing up 150 girls. 'Girls' covered a large age range – 18 to 60 – but the NAAFI roles were deliberately aimed at the younger age group, with publicity stating that 'the activities of NAAFI are widespread, offering a life full of interest, especially to girls with a spice of adventure in their make-up.'[12]

When women were allowed to start studying at Oxford University, and female-only colleges were established, it created a burgeoning job market for women, too. Lodging houses for female students emerged – 40-year-old Caroline Allen ran a university lodging house on the High Street in 1911, for example, as did Alice Davis, 41, and 66-year-old Caroline Bennett. These houses enabled single and widowed women to run a business from their own homes, giving them company and an income. Married women helped run lodging houses for students with their husbands. If you had a spare room or two, and needed additional income, opening your house up as a university lodging house, or advertising 'rooms' or 'apartments' for students and visitors was a good way of getting income and having company and conversation. On a smaller scale, one 'lady, occupying a larger house than she requires' simply advertised for a 'lady to board and reside with her. No children.' Here, a combination of economy and company was clearly in play.[13]

Women were also needed to help maintain the colleges, working as cooks, housemaids, kitchenmaids and pantry maids for the individual college. In 1911, Jessie Giles, a 27-year-old housemaid, signed the census form for Somerville College, recording the girls who worked there; the youngest was Edith Lily May Drew, a 14-year-old college pantry maid. Meanwhile, at Lady Margaret Hall, the oldest member of domestic staff was Eleanor Hales, the 38-year-old cook, and the youngest was housemaid Elizabeth Arlett, aged 16. Many of these workers were local to Oxford, understandably as they would still live with their families, as 'living-out' staff, living-in domestic staff reducing in number in the twentieth century.

One of the significant employers in Oxford was, and is, the Oxford University Press, which had first been established in the sixteenth century. From the late nineteenth century, the OUP expanded significantly, opening overseas offices, and employing an increasing number of people. These included print shop workers and messengers, and included both girls and women.[14] In 1911, 17-year-old Ada Lucy Rawlins Inn,[15] the daughter of a bricklayer, was working in the university press's warehouse, while 13-year-old Vera Webb, 14-year-old Jennie Stone and 15-year-old Hilda Cook all gave their occupations as 'gatherers' there – gathering up the pages of books. In 1881, Mary Shirley, 19, said that she was a 'taker off' at the OUP. Many of the city's young women, from working-class and artisan households, were employed in these menial capacities at the press, enabling them to make a valued contribution to the family income.

However, the city has long been associated with the university and, as the previous chapter showed, once the university had opened up to female students, many went on to become university staff themselves. The other common profession for those women at the university was to become a teacher, if only for a few years – say, before marrying or moving to another job – and a university-level education was seen as a means of gaining a good teaching position. Other women set up their own schools, such as the Misses Hooper's Crescent Lodge School for girls, which employed numerous 'masters' in various subjects, including Monsieur Manier of the Academie de Douai Université in France to teach both French and German, Signor Tivoli to teach Italian, and Monsieur D'Egville as the dancing and calisthenics teacher.[16] The Misses Hooper were proud of their foreign staff and their references, who were largely vicars and solicitors, a solidly middle-class clientele. They took both day pupils – at a charge of four guineas a term – and boarders.[17]

If one was educated, but poor, a genteel and respectable situation was that of the governess. The governess occupied an awkward position within a family – she wasn't viewed by servants as one of them; but neither was she part of the family. As Bonnie Smith has noted, 'she was ... that most unfortunate individual: the single, middle-class woman who had to earn her own living.... Her presence created practical difficulties within the Victorian home because she was neither a servant nor a member of the family.'[18] Her social class was more similar to the family employing her than to the class of the domestic servants, so she could find herself alone and friendless in her job. However, it was also a job deemed to be suitable for a respectable young girl, and offered her that paternalistic protection that women were seen to need if they were working outside of the family home.

The local papers abound with advertisements for governess positions, such as the one in the *Oxford Journal* in 1876, placed by a woman living at 12 Park Terrace:

> A Young Lady, having a few hours to spare daily, is desirous of a re-engagement as Governess; a private family preferred. Highest testimonials.[19]

These testimonials – references – were vital to a young woman wanting a good position. In the same issue of the *Oxford Journal*, another advertisement stated:

> The widow of a clergyman wishes to recommend her late Governess. She is 22, and teaches good English, French, German, and Drawing, with Elementary Music and Latin.[20]

There was competition for good governess positions, and the securing of a positive testimonial from a respectable family would improve one's chances of being employed over a less experienced girl, or one with less fulsome references. As the century neared its end, and girls were able to sit their school examinations, and take part in university courses (even if they weren't still allowed to gain a degree), their academic experience and qualifications were increasingly used as a selling point, with governesses highlighting their Local Examinations successes, and attendance at Oxford.

Even to be a nursery governess in the 1920s, an Oxford certificate and teaching experience could be specified by employers. Governesses increasingly specified wanting positions that were daily or weekly, not living-in, long-term jobs. One girl in 1903 stated that she wanted to work as a daily or weekly governess in or near Oxford, and could offer tuition in French, music and drawing in return.[21] Both girls and employers could be choosy. One girl in 1875 stated that she would only consider jobs as a daily governess to pupils under 12 as she had experience in educating this age; but immediately above her advert was one from a 'C.B.R' in Oxford, wanting 'a lady to instruct one or two children, about the age of twelve, five hours daily, Music, French, Drawing and Latin required.' Another woman placed an advert wanting 'a young lady, as governess, to instruct a little girl nine years of age, in general English with music, and assist in the care of a younger child.' Sometimes, there was little difference between a governess and a general mother's help.[22]

Although some girls felt confident enough to be very specific about the type of work they wanted, others had to be more flexible about what work they would take on – teaching or governessing were options rather than something the individual desperately wanted to do as a career. One lady living in Oxford made this clear when she stated that she was looking for employment for a few hours each day, offering her services as 'reading, secretarial work, lessons in English, French, German, arithmetic and elementary Latin.'[23] Others were flexible about whether they taught in a school as a teacher, or as a governess for a family. One woman – known by the initials C.M.G. – who advertised for a governess position in 1881 stated:

> A Lady, who has had experience in first-class schools and in a private family, desires an engagement as daily or resident governess in Oxford or the neighbourhood. Excellent references. Age 23.[24]

Teaching commonly required knowledge of subjects such as English, maths, and languages, but other, more social, skills were also needed for those from the middle and upper classes.

These, too, were teaching jobs that women as well as men could undertake. Mrs Henry Webb (née Elizabeth Stacey) held dancing and calisthenics classes for the gentry in Oxford in the 1880s, promoting her ability to teach the newest and most popular dances.[25]

Servants were also needed for domestic settings, as well as for the university, hotels, shops and businesses. The constant need for servants created other job opportunities for women – in 1902, for example, Teresa Bates ran a 'select' registry for male and female servants from her home at 6 New Road. She prided herself on giving 'special personal attention to ladies' and servants' requirements', and she charged nothing to those servants who signed up with her until they had been engaged.[26] Similarly, Mrs Holton had an 'old-established' agency on Walton Street, with a London branch too, boasting that vacancies were 'always too numerous' to specify in the press.[27] On the same road, at number 32, Mrs King had a 'well-known' registry, and advertised her services, stating:

> Servants! Servants!! Numbers always wanted. Good situations. High wages. Personal attention to all applicants, and every care given to suit all classes comfortably and well. No fee till engaged. Offices and interviewing-rooms on ground floor. Trams from the town pass the door.[28]

And a third woman, Miss Walter, ran her 'City and County Registry' from 4 Magdalen Street, but unlike Mrs King, was happy to detail specific vacancies in the press, such as an experienced parlourmaid and a cook wanted for a property in North Oxford, each on a salary of £30 a year, to reflect their prior experience.[29]

Not all households would use an agency as an intermediary, of course; many individuals would simply place an advertisement in the press themselves, stating what they needed, or look for out of work servants' adverts for situations. Many domestic households sought a general servant who could also cook – 'plain cooking' often being specified, and 'no children' would also be stated, meaning that the servant would not be required to take on any childcare issues ('no washing' was also sometimes stated). These adverts declined from around the First World War period, as war and its aftermath created social change. It became rarer for the average family to employ a servant, and even the larger, grand houses in the city might make do with fewer, if any, staff. Times were changing, and girls in service now increasingly sought and gained work in other fields.

In conclusion, women had long had jobs in Oxford, but the increasing desire to consume, to buy produce, in the second half of the nineteenth century led to more opportunities for women to take on businesses. In 1869, for example, Miss Jane Drinkwater was operating a baker's on Charles Street, and Mrs Ellen Brookes was working as ironmonger and cutler, based at 20 Paradise Street. Florence Tyson Brazier was a music seller and stationer at 109 High Street, and in a similar occupation, sisters Susan and Elizabeth Baxter were working as printers and publishers at 89 St Aldate's.

These women were from different backgrounds and of varied marital statuses. Florence Tyson Brazier, for example, was a 23-year-old single woman from the Holywell parish of central Oxford, the daughter of wine merchant Charles Tyson Brazier and his wife, the former Sarah Esther Prior – and granddaughter of John Prior, the butler at Brasenose College (he is also variously referred to in the historical record as Brasenose's purveryor or manciple). Susan and Elizabeth Baxter were two of the daughters of printer and bookseller William Baxter, a widower; in 1861, he had four unmarried daughters living with him at 89 St Aldate's; the three older girls, Anne, Mary and Susan, aged then between 36 and 43, were working as governesses, whereas the youngest, Elizabeth, 34, was housekeeper for her father. William Baxter died in 1865, and so then the housekeeper and one of the governesses took on his business and continued operating it from the family home. In a similar situation, Florence Tyson Brazier's father had died in 1860, so perhaps she had been left money and set up a business to generate a long-term income.

At the turn of the twentieth century, a similar diversity of occupations held by women was evident, as a study of local trade and street directories shows. In the 1903 Kelly's Directory, dressmakers such as Eliza Nickols on George Street were still well represented; but of her neighbours, Mrs Eliza Hewlett worked as a pastry cook, Mrs Elizabeth Scott as a confectioner, Mrs Jane Taylor as a beer retailer, and Mrs Eliza Hughes had her own shop, while in Corn Exchange Buildings, Miss Fanny Harris ran a restaurant.[30] Four years later, Miss Amelia Matthews worked as a court dressmaker at 10 Beaumont Street, while Mary Ann Elizabeth May ran a dairy on Little Clarendon Street, Florence Mortimer a shop on Hythe Bridge Street, Jane Mulcock a shop on Walton Crescent, and Adeline Narroway a shop at 72 St Clement's Street.

Many of the occupations these women had were domestic in some form or other – making and selling food and drink (the subject of the next chapter) or making clothes, for example; another common occupation of local women was to rent their spare rooms out, either as 'apartments' or as university lodgings. They used what they had, whether in terms of skills or housing, to make money and gain some independence. Some were married, others widowed or single, and in need of income. Some women might work just for a while, whereas others had long careers. However, it is sometimes difficult to ascertain just how much women worked, and for how long. In terms of the census – a key archival records in analysing occupation and households – a married woman might not be deemed to have a 'proper' occupation outside of domestic duties.

Rosina Papel, née Whitman, listed as a wardrobe dealer in the 1907 Kelly's Directory, had no occupation listed for her in either the 1901 or the 1911 censuses. By 1911, had she given up her job, or was it simply that the census enumerator only recorded her husband Eli's job as a tailor, and not any other role she had beyond being Eli's wife? Alternatively, she may have worked for a while when her younger child, Reginald, was small, to help the household income, but had given up by 1911– Reginald was 12 then, and not be far off leaving school and working himself. It seems likely that many women worked in some capacity or another, but that some worked for their husbands or fathers and thus had no occupation listed in the census – such as in pubs, where the father was the landlord, but enlisted his wife and daughters to serve as barmaids – or that others only worked for spells where they or their families needed extra income. What we see represented in the trade directories therefore represents only part of Oxford women's employment – but what it does show is that women were resourceful and industrious, and that they used their existing skills to make money.

As the century moved on, new job opportunities opened up for local women. By the 1930s, for example, women were working as bookkeepers – as can be seen from the Clarendon Hotel's employment of two females in this role – and as shorthand typists. Betty Carter, 25, was working as both shorthand typist and bookkeeper in 1939, being employed at a grocery and provisions store at 55 Cornmarket Street. Gladys Adams, meanwhile, was a glove machinist – a modern, mechanised, version of the glovers whose industry had centred around various Oxfordshire towns nearly a century earlier. But one thing remained consistent over the period – women worked, and worked in many different occupations. They were a vital part of Oxford's economy and daily life.

CHAPTER THREE

Home

Home was a concept that meant different things to different people, and as was often the case in the nineteenth and early twentieth centuries, a lot depended on what your economic background was. For the poor, the struggle to keep a roof over one's head was a constant and real pressure; and even for the upper classes, finances could take a tumble due to bad investments, with bankruptcy sometimes resulting. Homes were more commonly leased or rented rather than bought in the Victorian era – the house-buying nation that we are today is a relatively modern phenomenon. Council housing as we know it is a post-First World War concept; prior to this, the poorer members of society were reliant on other forms of 'help'.

In 1834, the Poor Law Amendment Act had been passed in England, which led to the establishment of workhouses to house the indigent and poor. Workhouses had existed before this, but organised by parish; from 1834, Poor Law Unions were set up that covered several parishes or smaller areas. In Oxford, the situation was slightly different from many other areas. In 1771, eleven of the city's parishes had been legally incorporated, meaning that it was the Incorporation that had the power to assess the poor rate and run a House of Industry.[1] This was duly built in the area now covered by Wellington Square. The parish of St Giles came outside the incorporated area and had its own workhouse at Summertown. When the 1834 Act was passed, Oxford was largely exempt from its provisions, and refused to convert to a Poor Law Union, despite the best attempts of the Poor Law Commission. The Incorporation agreed to include the parish of St John the Baptist within its metaphorical walls, but rejected appeals to also include St Giles and St Clement's, who then formed their own Poor Law Union. The Incorporation of Oxford continued until 1926, and so led to nearly a century of parts of the city dealing with paupers one way, while other external but local parishes formed separate Poor Law Unions and as such ran their own workhouses.[2]

The old Oxford workhouse continued in operation until 1859, and included rooms for elderly women, a mangle room and oakum room – where inmates would have to undertake work – an apothecary's shop and brewhouse, and a laundry and drying room. Female residents were usually required to undertake the washing and drying of clothing within the workhouse. When the original workhouse was sold off, a new site at the north of Cowley Road was purchased from Pembroke and Magdalen colleges – the new buildings were built between 1863 and 1865.[3] This new building had provision for the elderly poor to have their own dayrooms and bedrooms, and for married couples to reside together. The paupers inside still had to undertake work if they were fit enough – primarily either picking oakum, or crushing and bagging gypsum. The building was gradually extended over the course of the century and by 1908, over 12,000 tramps were using its casual wards over the course of the year.

During the First World War, the workhouse became a hospital treating war casualties, and so the workhouse paupers had to go to other institutions around Oxford. In 1929, under the Local Government Act, the City Council took over the workhouse's operation, and it became what was known as a 'Public Assistance Institution'. Following the Second World War, it became a hospital specialising in geriatric care.[4]

In 1881, the census recorded the inmates of the Oxford Workhouse on Cowley Road, and it showed that many of the residents came from outside the city; they had presumably moved to the city some years earlier in search of better work, or more opportunities than the places they had come from. One local woman who had become impoverished was Frances Adams, then aged in her 80s, who had previously been a laundress.[5] Another Oxford local who had been sent to the workhouse was 69-year-old Emma Blay, a former domestic servant who was described in the census as an imbecile – a broad description that could cover a wide range of mental health issues or learning disabilities. But many other female inmates came from further afield – Berkshire, Suffolk, London, Surrey – all drawn to Oxford either for work or for love, but who had found themselves impoverished and in need of financial help. Whole families could be sent to the workhouse; in other cases, an elderly mother and her middle-aged daughter (such as appears to be the case with Ann Day, a 71-year-old charwoman from Oxford, who was in the workhouse with 48-year-old servant Maria Day). All ages saw poverty – from 78-year-old tailoress Catherine Farmer, to 33-year-old servant Ann Ely.

In the late nineteenth and very early twentieth centuries, some forms of what we today call social housing did start to emerge in Britain, as well as workers' housing built in communities such as Saltaire and Bournville. These earlier units, tenements, were built in inner city areas such as London and Manchester, and foresaw the slum clearances and estate building of the first decades of the twentieth century. In Oxford, some council houses started to be built in Headington from 1920, when twenty-four houses on Bullington Road were built by Messrs Benfield and Loxley. By 1930, over 300 council houses had been completed on the Gipsy Lane estate; but council housing in Oxford only really increased in the years following the Second World War, when there was a severe local housing shortage.[6] The first residents moved into the large housing estate at Blackbird Leys – which consisted of nearly 3,000 dwellings – in 1953.[7]

Of course, not all women during this era faced poverty, but in a city like Oxford, there were clear differences between the wives of academics and, as time went on, female academics themselves, who were often from well-to-do backgrounds and lived comfortably – and those from humbler backgrounds, who lacked the same level of education and opportunity. These latter might just about cope for a while, but then a change in circumstance – the death of a partner, the loss of an income – might leave them in dire straits. In the days before the NHS, income support, housing benefit, and the like, the workhouse was often the only thing standing between them and destitution.

For those more fortunate, life was very different, as the grand Victorian and Edwardian houses in north Oxford, for example, are testament to. These were homes that required extensive decoration and furnishings, servants to maintain them, cooks to create laborious meals in the kitchens. The Victorian wife would oversee these servants, and often undertake the household accounts, leaving her husband to work. Childcare might well be delegated to a nanny or other staff member; dinner parties would be organised, and there would be other local women to call on during the day. As the twentieth century progressed, however, the dynamics of family changed, and home life became more egalitarian. After the First World War, the number of servants employed by families started to reduce, with more women undertaking the household tasks previously done by servants.

The idea was promoted, through books and newspapers in the nineteenth and into the twentieth century, that the goal of young women should not be work, but a respectable marriage. Although many women remained single, whether through choice or necessity, or because of a lack of prospects, the word 'spinster' had, and arguably still does have, a negative connotation. The ideal home, it was implied, consisted of a husband, wife, children and servants. Every self-respecting middle-class couple would consider placing an advertisement in the newspapers to mark their engagement or marriage. This was the case throughout the period studied here, from the marriage of William Howland, a Thame mason, and Elizabeth Watts, in Oxford in October 1851, to the wedding of Margaret Nowell Smith and Theodore Richard 'Dick' Milford, who married at St Margaret's Church in Oxford in 1937.[8] This latter couple's marriage was noted in the *Western Gazette*, because the bride was the daughter of the former headmaster of Sherborne School; although the groom, Dick, was son of the late housemaster of the same school.⁹ Many of these marriages must have been perfectly happy, no doubt; but divorce records and newspaper reports also highlight that for others, marriage could be problematic at best, and utterly miserable at worst.

Prior to 1857, divorce was out of bounds for all but the wealthiest members of society, as it required a private Act of Parliament. However, the passing of the Matrimonial Causes Act in that year opened divorce up to other classes; although it still cost money to bring a divorce petition to the courts, it was more affordable than previous methods, and records show that even those from fairly humble backgrounds used the divorce courts from this time. Divorce was, though, fundamentally a product of the patriarchal society of Victorian Britain. Whereas men could seek a divorce from their wives on the grounds of adultery, wives had to find proof of a second 'offence' – such as neglect, desertion, or marital violence. Bringing evidence of affairs or bad behaviour to the court meant often salacious stories that the newspapers eagerly recounted for their readers.

Not all divorces involved detailed accounts of adultery, but many did. One of these detailed accounts involved the 1892 divorce petition of Walter Biggs, who sought a divorce from his wife, Lavinia Jane (née Baker). The couple had been married back in 1876. Walter worked as a stationer at 8 Queen Street, Oxford, and the couple lived at 16 The Terrace, with their only child, Lavinia Agnes, born in 1879. After a few years of marriage, Walter discovered that Lavinia had a beautiful singing voice, and the couple decided she should go abroad to study music. In this, Walter was a very modern man, recognising his wife's talent and encouraging it. Mrs Biggs duly went off to study in Italy and France, under respected teachers, with her husband visiting her regularly. Mrs Biggs eventually became a singer, but performed at musical parties and at private houses, rather than professionally at public concerts. In 1892, however, Mr Biggs visited Durrant's Hotel, in Marylebone, and saw his wife there. On asking a waiter if he knew her, he was told that the previous year, she had stayed at the hotel for a week with a man, registering as 'Mr and Mrs G.B. Rodgers'. Mr Biggs' patience had worn thin, and he sought a divorce – although his solicitor noted that he could not ask 'Mr Rodgers' to pay the costs of the case, as 'it was not known who or where he was now'.[10]

It is not surprising, to modern readers, to learn that Lavinia had struggled to cope with the expectations of her society in terms of marital conformity. At the time of her wedding, she was just 16 years old, whereas her new husband was three decades older and had already been widowed twice. She was therefore very young and inexperienced, and went from a secure London upbringing with her family to being a wife and stepmother in Oxford – her husband already had four children from his two former wives. It is perhaps in recognition of her youth that her husband agreed for her to train as a singer, acting in more of a paternal role than that of a spouse; but it is perhaps also inevitable that her eyes were opened to the possibilities of life once she started travelling around Europe training, and she started to desire more than the life of a provincial stationer.

Prior to 1857, many couples would have stayed unhappily married, or informally separated – with many living separately whether by agreement or due to the 'abandonment' or desertion of one partner by the other. The desertion by men often left women struggling to feed children and unable to work because of childcare issues – or certainly, not able to do a job that would pay enough to maintain her and her family. This would lead to the involvement of the parish authorities, who could then seek to have the errant partner charged with desertion and ordered to pay maintenance to his family – if he could be tracked down. In other cases, men might travel some distance away from the family home in search of work, and again go missing. Despite technology improving, it can still be surprising as to how many of these men could be tracked down across the country.

In 1910, Henry Sheppard, a former reader at the Oxford University Press, then aged 48, asked for a divorce from his wife Louisa, alleging an affair with Hugh Godwin, who had been a member of staff with the National Telephone Company in the city. Louisa did not deny the facts, but argued that Henry had 'connived' in the affair, as well as delaying in bringing the divorce suit. It was heard in court that the Sheppards had married at the church of St Mary the Virgin on the High Street in September 1888. Henry had then been 26, his bride 24.

After their marriage, they lived at the King's Arms Hotel, which was run by Louisa's father, William. The papers stated that the couple helped him with the hotel management, but in reality, Henry continued to work as a compositor or printer, and the 1891 census records Louisa as the manageress of the hotel. When William Franklin died in 1897, his daughter and son-in-law moved into their own home at Beechcroft Road, and a former resident, Hugh Godwin, became their lodger. One day in January 1898, Louisa went to London stating that she was going to deal with matters relating to her father's estate. The following day she announced that she was not returning home. Henry 'made enquiries' and traced Louisa and Hugh to Brighton. Hugh admitted that Louisa was 'under his protection' because 'yourself and your society are distasteful to her, and she does not wish to have anything more to do with you'. Henry argued that he had not been able to embark on a divorce case at that point because of his lack of money. Louisa later gave birth to a child by Godwin, but by 1901 he had left her, and she was pleading forgiveness to her still financially embarrassed husband.[11] It was only in 1910 that he was finally able to ask for a divorce.[12]

Although many of these divorces offered couples a way out of an unhappy marriage for both of them, it is clear that the affairs of wives were what made the cases newsworthy. Women expressed their dissatisfaction and need for romance, for love, through new relationships, and were able to behave as clandestinely and secretively as husbands could. In some cases, it can be seen that the couple appeared quite disparate, and that their marriages were, in some ways, doomed to go wrong – as in the case of Walter Biggs, a 47-year-old widowed father marrying a 16-year-old girl. But in other cases, men brought malicious actions in order to publicly embarrass their wives. In one 1923 case, Henry Barrett of St Clement's had asked for a divorce from his wife, Florence, on the grounds of her adultery with a police court missionary and probation officer named Henry

Ferris Pike. Both Pike and Mrs Barrett denied this. The Barretts had married just five years earlier, but soon separated due to frequent disagreements. Mrs Barrett had gone to work as a housekeeper to Mr Pike, both at Greyfriars in Oxford, and in Harrogate. She stated very firmly that while working for Mr Pike, she had slept each night at her parents' house. Their landlady in Harrogate also gave evidence stating that there had been 'no impropriety between the parties' there. The judge in the case stated that there was not a single 'shred' of evidence showing that Mrs Barrett had done anything wrong, and that 'the only thing that came out clearly was that the petitioner [Mr Barrett] was acting purely out of spite'.[13]

The divorce cases show the limited options open to a married woman if she was unhappy, despite the passing of the 1857 Matrimonial Causes Act. The Act put the onus on women to get proof not only of adultery but also of cruelty, whereas a husband only had to find proof of the adultery. It also still required the money to hire a solicitor and produce a petition for divorce. With many women dependent on their husband's income, they might not have been able to do so, and so either endure an unhappy marriage, or embark on an affair – or simply disappear.

Another option was simply not to marry, and many women remained single, either through choice, through lack of money or opportunity, or failing to meet the right man. Some single women took on the traditional domestic responsibilities of a wife but for another family member, thus giving them the security of home and companionship. Walter Biggs, the husband abandoned by his younger wife, had at least four children by his first wife – Herbert W. Biggs, Walter Lyle Biggs, Helen Gaskell Biggs, and Sidney Biggs.[14] Walter – an organist and music teacher – never married, but instead, his spinster sister Helen became his housekeeper at 30 Argyle Street, until her death at the age of 70 in 1934. Walter died six years later, aged 82.

As these cases might suggest, there have always been different families with different values coexisting in Oxford, as elsewhere; with the Roaring Twenties creating a modern society where sex, music, dancing and the like were seen as fundamental parts of an enjoyable life for the young, the church became increasingly concerned about what messages were being put out to society. Canon L.W. Grensted gave a talk in Oxford in the summer of 1933 where he discussed sex and procreation, arguing that although a marriage without children wasn't ideal, neither was the concept of a large, Victorian, family: 'it is a rather ludicrous idea that every family should have just as many children as possible.'[15]

As the Second World War progressed, some individuals became increasingly concerned by the impact of war on ordinary family life. Many fathers, husbands and sons were away fighting; if they came back, they might be greatly changed either physically or mentally, and families might struggle either with living without the male head of their family, or struggle to readjust once that individual returned. In July 1941, the Women's Public Health Officers' Association held a conference at Oxford, with one speaker, Agnes Crosthwaite – honorary secretary of the British Federation of Social Workers – commenting that there was a 'deeply emotional conflict' taking place among families as a result of the war. It was said that parental control had slackened to the extent that children were arriving late at school, they were badly dressed, and dirtier than before; yet it was not believed that economic pressure was to blame for this. Authority was perceived to be breaking down; if teachers complained to parents about their children's lateness or behaviour, the parents responded with abuse. It was also speculated that individuals were getting fat 'because of the feeling of security that shelters gave them, and because of the extra sleep they were able to obtain there'. Putting on weight and being complacent were seen as bad traits during war time. Yet it was also recognised that children responded 'calmly' to the upheaval of war, taking their siblings to shelters with little fuss or panic.[16]

In other areas, some better-off Oxford families were prepared to help others less fortunate than themselves, while also improving their own home lives. In 1912, for example, Henry Cooper, a tutor at Keble College, advertised in the *Army and Navy Gazette*, stating that he desired the 'charge of two or three children as companions to his own two little girls'. His youngest, Audrey, was not that little – she would have been around 13 at the time he placed the advert.[17] An older daughter, May Frideswyde Bickersteth Cooper, was then 18. The other 'little girl' he was referring to was unlikely, then, to be May; however, in 1911, he had been looking after another girl around the same age as his daughter Audrey, one Bertha White Conway, who was originally from Burton-on-Trent in Staffordshire, and so he might have meant her. It suggests that this may not have been the first time he had advertised for company.

He emphasised that he was married, with a wife experienced with children, stressing that his advert was above board. He had a 'large airy house and garden' and already kept a French children's maid; there would be, he stated, 'good educational advantages' to the children coming to his home.[18] Given that he was advertising on the same page as an advert for a fund for seamen's widows and orphans, it is clear that there was a need to help parentless children, and a desire by some in Oxford to help them. Presumably his wife, Anna Maria, had been consulted and was fully on-board with the potential additions to her household. Until her marriage, she had been Anna Maria Steward, the daughter of solicitor Edward Steward. Born in 1858, she had been married by her father-in-law in Norfolk on 1 July 1891. She had been, then, from a comfortable, middle-class home in Norfolk, and married into a similar one. However, she had also known loss; her father had died when she was fairly young (he being some twenty years older than her mother); although her mother had been left financially secure, living in The Hall in Saxlingham Nethergate, Norfolk, Anna Maria was one of several siblings, and must have grown up in a noisy household. Given these facts, perhaps the desire to have more children come into her home once her daughters were growing up, originated with her. She could recreate the large family of her own childhood, give her daughters more company, and help, perhaps, a couple of less fortunate children in the process. However, there is no archival evidence for whether the newspaper advert was successful or not. Anna Maria died in 1924 at the Regents Palace Hotel in London, some nine years prior to her husband.

The case studies used in this chapter hopefully illustrate the sheer variety of existence in the city and its environs over the course of the last couple of centuries. Much of the focus of Oxford history has been on the lives of those involved with the university, yet the city was very much town as well as gown, with poor and rich, working class and upper class living in close proximity to each other, yet having very different lives. Certain aspects of life had a commonality to them – relationships could be complex in every setting; and death visited all classes of family, with children from richer families dying, as did those from poorer, certainly throughout the nineteenth century. Look, for example, at the Bracher family; Edward Bracher was one of the city's pioneering photographers, living in middle class, prosperous surroundings on the Banbury Road with his wife Susanna and their two children – Edward and Rosa. Yet in 1872, they lost their son, then aged 22, when he collapsed and died during a run with friends near Wolvercote; just two years later, their daughter Rosa, aged 23, died of tuberculosis.[19] The couple lived for many years in their large house without either of the children they must have thought would look after them into their old age.[20]

CHAPTER FOUR

Food & Drink

Throughout this period Oxford was somewhere visitors wanted to come and stay. These were not just holidaymakers, or relatives of those men – and later women – studying at the university, but travellers and businesspeople too. To cater for them were hotels and other lodgings, vying with each other to provide comfortable accommodation and meals for their weary lodgers. These establishments needed staff to help – even the smaller places had one or more servants, and larger ones needed even more. Advertisements placed in the local press were able to specify the gender of staff wanted, and even their marital status; one advert, from 1905, advertised for a woman to bake bread on the premises, adding 'widow with child would suit'.[1] Someone with sole responsibility for a child was seen to be likely to stay for a while, and be both responsible and sensible. Back in 1853, another advert placed by the management of a hotel in Oxford asked for a 'respectable woman' to apply for a job as an upper chambermaid, joining two others; it also needed a second 'respectable woman' to be a kitchenmaid, as well as a man to work as an under-waiter. Fearing fake references, it asked that only those with 'undeniable reference' apply.[2]

Arguably Oxford's most famous hotel, then as now, was the Randolph, on the corner of Magdalen and Beaumont Streets. Building began in 1864, and the hotel opened two years later, on Tuesday, 13 February 1866, marking its official opening with an inaugural dinner in the hotel's 'splendid coffee room'.

The *Oxford Times* reported on its opening by saying that 'dinner was served in a style of elegance that has rarely been excelled', and that 'the minutest details which could in any way add to the comfort and happiness of the guests had been most carefully studied and supplied'.[3] However, good press was not limited to the local paper, partly because the hotel advertised its facilities across the country. One advert placed in the *Cambridge Independent Press* by its secretary and manager, George Curtis, stated that the 'recently erected' hotel 'is now open for the reception of Families and Visitors; Wedding Breakfasts, Dinners, &c supplied. Wines of all kinds may be had from the Company's Wholesale Cellars.'[4] This was not a hotel that aimed to cater for the lower classes or the poor.

To serve and cater for these elegant guests with ample wallets were both men and women, undertaking a range of tasks from being a knife or plate man to a linen keeper, a messenger or a porter. Some specific roles were seen as female only, such as the chambermaid and kitchenmaid. In 1911, the census recorded 20-year-old Eva Townley, an Oxford native, as one of the hotel's chambermaids. Although many of the staff came from Oxford or the wider county, some were drawn from further afield, such as 32-year-old linen keeper Agnes Ingsaw, who was originally from Glasgow. All ages could find work at the Randolph; from Eva and another chambermaid and Oxford-native Lilian Louisa Goodall, both 20, to their fellow chambermaid, 66-year-old Susannah Reeves Strange. Such jobs were for unmarried women, and so when Lilian Goodall, a tailor's daughter, married 'public servant' James John Timothy Harrison in 1920, a firm line was drawn through the 'rank or profession' box next to her name and marital status on her marriage entry in the register of St Margaret's in North Oxford. Both Lilian and her new husband were 29 when they married, suggesting that both had worked until they had sufficient money to start their married life – it would have taken Lilian some time as a chambermaid to accumulate sufficient savings.

The Randolph was not the only hotel in town, although it may have been the grandest. Oxford was also home to a temperance hotel – Dodson's – and in 1902, it was advertising for 'a respectable girl, 18 to 29, as chambermaid and waitress'.[5] The temperance movement had some success in Oxford; as well as Dodson's, there was also the Oxford Café No. 3, at 84 St Aldate's, which advertised itself in 1881 as a 'family, commercial and temperance hotel, dining and refreshment rooms'. It encouraged choirs, bible classes and school parties who might be visiting Oxford to come for refreshments 'at moderate prices'; these refreshments included ham and beef sandwiches, hot joints for lunch from 12 p.m. until 2 p.m., and, of course, 'all kinds of temperance drinks', which included ginger ale, lemonade, soda and seltzer, as well as 'Bechett's Fruit Syrup'.[6] As might be expected from the temperance movement in an academic city, the café saw the university's students as in need of its intervention, and highlighted its proximity both to Christ Church college and to the river, where boating parties might be headed.

By the 1930s, some things had changed in terms of the jobs held by women in hotels. At the Clarendon Hotel on Cornmarket Street, in early 1939, women still worked as the hotel's barmaids, chambermaids and housekeeper – the latter position being occupied by 29-year-old Phyllis Neville (later Phyllis Locke). However, Eileen Driscoll (later Farrando), aged 19, was employed as a bookkeeper there, as was 54-year-old Alice Smith who, during the war, also acted as an Air Raid Precautions (ARP) warden for the City of Oxford. Key, though, was the management. Cyril Davy, aged 36, was the hotel and catering manager, listed alongside and equal to his wife Dorothy, the hotel's manageress. Both worked for the ARP during the war, Cyril as a warden and Dorothy as a business warden.

Away from the hotels, the British public house was a centuries-old institution – somewhere where locals and visitors alike could get food, drink, and conversation. Unsurprisingly, Oxford was home to many inns and taverns, and there were often girls behind the bar serving. Such girls were often part of the landlord's family – with all members of his household expected to help out the family business. They didn't always get their contributions recognised, although sometimes the census returns record women's work in pubs. For example, the 1911 census notes Oxford-born Laura

Appleton's job as 'assists in public house', the pub being run by her husband; however, a Mrs Bell, living at the High Street pub run by her husband the same year, had no occupation given. Did she really not help him in his business at all? It seems unlikely, but if she made a contribution, it was not recorded by the authorities.

Some smaller establishments, as well as pubs, doubled up in purpose, offering both refreshments and accommodation in a few rooms above the main premises. One of the most well-known early twentieth century Oxford cafes was the Victoria Coffee House, located on the corner of St Clements Street and Boulter Street. This was originally built as a Working Men's Institute, and had become a café by the end of the 1880. One report from 1894 states that the café was under the management of a C. Molyneux, who also worked as a local football secretary; this may have been Charles Molyneux, who for many years worked as a beer retailer further down the road at 76 St Clements Street.[7] However, around the turn of the century, Walter and Emma Hazell took on the café – Walter as proprietor and Emma as its manageress. An advertisement from the early years of the twentieth century states that there was 'good and reasonable accommodation for cyclists and commercials [commercial travellers], boarders taken'.[8]

The exact date that the Hazells took on the Victoria Coffee House is not known. The couple only married in January 1901, when Walter gave his occupation as a police constable, and two months later, when the 1901 census was taken, Walter was a general labourer on the Headington Hill Hall estate, living in an estate lodge with Emma. Walter's obituary in the Oxford Times in 1938, however, suggested that he had been running the café for 33 years – in other words, since 1905.[9] The Hazells were certainly there by 1911, when the census recorded them both at the Victoria Coffee House, together with their 1-year-old daughter Edith Mary, two boarders and one maid. As the Victoria Coffee House had always done, with the Hazells in charge, the premises continued to host local societies and clubs for their meetings; for example, in 1904, the annual general meeting of the Victoria Cricket Club was held one evening at the coffee house.[10] It also hosted more progressive meetings; in 1899, the Oxford District branch of the AOF (the Ancient Order of Foresters, a friendly society that aimed to care for the sick) met at the Victoria Coffee House to initiate ten new members and to hold a 'court' to decide whether to admit adult female members. This was agreed, and 'Sister Vallis' was elected as a court officer, with 'Sister Bulbeck' elected as secretary.[11] The Hazells continued to run the café until their deaths, which both came in 1938 – Emma in April that year, and her husband just over six months later.

The Victoria was operated around the same time as the Oxford Café and Dining Rooms at 3-4 Castle Street. Run by Anna Maria Jarvis in 1895, like the Victoria, it promoted its accommodation to cyclists, but also to 'parties', so presumably had a bit more room for accommodation than the Hazells' establishment. It offered bed and breakfast, hot joints for lunch, and 'dinners cut from the best English meat from 6d'. No alcohol was served; instead, there was tea, coffee, cocoa, 'minerals and syrups' – and there was also a large room that Mrs Jarvis let out for public meetings.[12] Dinners comprised meat with two vegetables or hot meat puddings with potatoes, but 'chops, steaks, soups, gravies, Melton Mowbray pies' were also on sale. A night in a well-aired bed cost a shilling.[13]

Little is known about this proprietress, although the café itself had a long history. In 1877, it had been run by George Busby, and in 1882, John Pill – who had previously run the Railway Café in Osney – took over. Initially, the Oxford Café was based just at 4 Castle Street.[14] A year later, it was being advertised as a temperance café and hotel, and although by Mrs Jarvis's time (she had become proprietress by January 1895), the temperance had disappeared from the café's name, and in January 1895 the sale of Kop's ale and stout was carried out from the premises, it later seems to have returned to being a 'dry' establishment.[15] Mrs Jarvis, however, doesn't appear to have had a long tenure. She was still there in November 1896, when she prosecuted Charles Whately, alias Lilley, a Kenilworth grape-grower, for obtaining food and lodging by false pretences, but in May 1898, John Pill had returned to run the Oxford Café again, now stressing his introduction of fried fish for dinner.[16] His first advert on returning to Castle Street noted that it would be 'opened on Saturday [14 May] by the old proprietor ... Mr John Pill (for fifteen years proprietor of the Oxford Café) has pleasure in announcing that he has again taken the management of the house'.[17] He did not state what had happened to Mrs Jarvis.

Women worked both as café proprietors and café waitresses. In this latter group was Edith Elsie Cook, who in 1911, aged 21, was working as a waitress in Oxford. This was seen as a good occupation for a lower middle class or artisan family; Edith's father was a wine maker, and her siblings worked as a grocer's assistant, upholsterer and a 'gatherer up' of pages for the university press. In the same year, 27-year-old Mildred Parsons was still living at home with her parents (her father being a woollen draper) at 43 Walton Crescent, but working as a restaurant waitress. Mabel Anne Savage, a 25-year-old woman living with her widowed mother in Marlborough Road, meanwhile, was working as a waitress in a hotel. The city's numerous eating establishments and hotels provided ample employment opportunities for unmarried girls who needed to help contribute to the household income, but who wanted something more than a life in service – but this career was also to decline over the first few decades of the twentieth century, due partly to the economic and social impact of First World War, leading women to seek different work opportunities to those that had been more prevalent in the mid-nineteenth century, for example. The popularity of waitressing as a job continued throughout the inter-war years, with it being increasingly common for married women to take on waitressing work.

The 1939 register records 132 women in the Oxford area who gave their occupation as waitress; forty-six women stated that they worked in local cafes – jobs that included clerking (doing the paperwork), being a counterhand, or a waitress. Sarah Catherine Lucy Brown, born in 1885, and living at 14a Broad Street in 1939, was proprietress of a café – as was the married Ellen Chiddington, living with her invalid husband John on the Cowley Road. In the same year as the 1939 Register was taken of the civilian population, Ellen's name also appeared in *Kelly's Directory*, listing her as

'Chiddington Ellen (Mrs), café, 250 Cowley Road'.[18] Today, the property is still a café.[19]

It has already been noted how the staff of Oxford store F. Cape & Co held their annual stocktaking party at the Cadena Café. The Cadena was part of a chain of coffee shops that had been established as Lloyd's Oriental Café in 1895. In 1907, the chain became known as Cadena Cafés, after the coffee blend it sold, and it eventually had over twenty branches. The Oxford branch of Lloyd's Oriental Café existed by 1902, but in 1928, the Cadena Café was opened at Cornmarket Street.[20] In the 1930s, this was renowned for its music, as well as for its coffee and doughnuts; in 1935, it had advertised for a 'brilliant cellist' (who would be at an advantage if he could also play sax or guitar) for a permanent job, under the supervision of the café's musical director.[21] It is no wonder that other local organisations and shops also held their events there, and that those from further afield made sure they stopped there on outings.

In 1930, the committee of the Bristol Shopkeepers' Protection and Benevolent Association had lunch at the Cadena Café on their outing, before heading to the Huntley and Palmer's biscuit factory in Reading, and in 1939, the women's section of the Dorchester-on-Thames British Legion branch held their annual dinner there.[22] The Cadena offered female performers the chance of work, such as Liverpool-based Molly McGrath – who played the cello, harp and banjo as well as being a singer – who was playing at the Cadena in November 1935.[23] This is, of course, in addition to the girls who took on waitressing work there, which involved working hours of 8.30 a.m. until 7.30 p.m. Monday to Saturday. There were perks for girls working at the Cadena, who were under the supervision of a female manageress; no Sunday working was required, the tips from customers could be good and they were given paid overtime.[24] In 1938, the Cadena Café advertised for a café supervisor: it was specified that this should be a 'young lady' of between 25 and 30 years of age, of 'good appearance and address', who should be experienced – in return, she would gain a 'progressive position'.[25]

Finally, no discussion of women's work in catering and related industries in Oxford can take place without mentioning the role of Sarah-Jane Cooper. Born Sarah-Jane Gill in Worcestershire in 1848, in 1872, she married Frank Cooper, who five years earlier had inherited his father's grocery at 83 High Street – the couple lived over the shop. In 1874, the then 24-year-old Sarah-Jane made some marmalade – some 76 lb worth, in fact – from her own recipe. Frank Cooper started to sell it to the public, with his wife making it behind the shop, and it proved very popular. In 1903, Cooper moved production to a new purpose-built factory at Park End Street. The building still exists as The Jam Factory, and the name of Frank Cooper's remains well-known; but Sarah-Jane's pivotal role in Cooper's success is perhaps less famous; indeed, none of the censuses during her married life list any occupation for her outside of her role of wife and mother.[26] As was often the case in Victorian England, wives worked behind the scenes, in an unpaid capacity, to support their husbands' business. They were often key to their husbands' success, but did not necessarily receive the credit.

These were women who worked in the hospitality trade; sometimes, as with Sarah-Jane Cooper, they had started making foodstuffs at home, for domestic use, but then branched out; others simply found employment within Oxford's many hotels and cafes. But when women needed to buy food and drink for their families, or female servants for their employers, what did they buy, and where from? Markets had been the traditional way for wives to purchase food, and Oxford's Covered Market – which is still operational today – opened in 1774, with the aim of creating a tidier city, as the outdoor market stalls were seen as 'untidy'. Previously, Oxford had been home to the likes of Fish Street (now St Aldate's) and Butcher Row (now Queen Street), their names evocatively referring to what their street markets focused on. The late eighteenth-century Oxford residents had come to see them as rather undesirable, smelly and messy areas, that restricted traffic along the roads. Once the Covered Market was built, no meat, fish, poultry, or vegetables were allowed to be sold on public streets.[27]

The desire to create a cleaner, more civilised city did not eradicate the previous noise of the old outdoor market; in 1879, for example, two fishmongers in the covered market were warned that they would lose their stalls if they did not behave in a quieter and more orderly manner – their shouting out the price and quality of their fish, to compete with each other, had annoyed other nearby stallholders.[28] A year later, one shop owner, Jesse Hughes, made a complaint against market stallholder John Scarrott, whose stall was opposite Hughes's two shops. Hughes had been affronted by the bad language frequently employed by Scarrott during the course of his business.[29]

Given this reputation in Victorian times for bad language and coarse behaviour, it seems likely that it would have been the working-class women and servants who would have used the market, rather than middle- or upper-class women, who would have left the purchasing of food to servants, or who would have had food delivered to their homes via servants' and tradesmen's entrances. But it would not have been a male environment, and many working-class women would have been able to hold their own against the stallholders' sales tactics.

In the nineteenth-century city, there was an increasing number of shops catering for every need, in every area – and food was no different. In the 1850s, the public could buy pig food from Messrs Seckham & Co at Friars Wharf, and at the other end of the scale, imported brandy at three shillings a bottle from wine merchant George Bruton on Queen Street. Meanwhile, Messrs Grimbly and Hughes, at 56 Cornmarket Street, offered tea and coffee for sale, among many other items.[30] The 1870s city directories give an indication of just how many businesses and trades were carried on in the city, from butchers, bakers and biscuit makers to confectioners such as Robert Wharton at 26 Cornmarket Street, and muffin and crumpet makers (Killpack's, at Littlegate Street, was one shop specialising in these items). Many shops combined different services or goods, so someone visiting William Way's shop at 120 St Aldate's, for example, could get their groceries but also their wine and spirits. Women were in business as well as being customers – a Mrs Turrill, possibly a relation of James Turrill, an Oxford poulterer, worked as a bacon curer in the city, for example, while a Mrs Trafford sold both beer and coal from a shop on Gas Street.[31] In 1876, one grocer and fruiterer listed in the trade directories for Oxford was Mrs E. H. Payne, based at 31 Broad Street; this was, in fact her husband's name, and Edward H. Payne had originally been the grocer at that premises, with his wife, Emily Ann Payne, taking over her husband's business after his death in the winter of 1871.[32]

In the second half of the nineteenth century, men vastly outnumbered women in the trade directories, and where women worked as food and drink retailers, they were primarily involved with selling beer, either from shops or as pub landladies. However, as is often the case with Victorian families, it is likely that many more women were involved in food and drink selling than were officially listed. Husbands and fathers may have run shops that women were involved in, either preparing goods for sale, or selling behind the counter. They were simply not recorded separately as being involved, although censuses may have described them as 'grocer's wife' or 'grocer's daughter'. These terms could mean that they were working with the male, but not always. The chances are, however, that every bit of help was appreciated – and expected – with small, family-run businesses.

Oxford was home to many eating establishments as well as places to buy food to eat later at home. The world wars saw usual practices disrupted; both world wars witnessed the introduction of food rationing. In the earlier stages of the First World War, rationing had been voluntary, with a system of compulsory rationing then imposed in stages during the winter of 1917. By the summer of 1918, ration books were being introduced to limit the amount of butter, meat and sugar individuals were able to purchase. This rationing was fairly short-lived compared to that of the Second World War, of course. Once again, the Germans attempted to restrict imports of food into Britain – which was largely dependent on the imports of certain goods such as sugar and cereals – by attacking ships. Faced with the prospect of food shortages, the Ministry of Food introduced a system of rationing, with those goods and foodstuffs rationed being extended over time. Oxford's residents had to register with shops and were given a ration book. The shopkeeper at their chosen shop would be given enough food to feed those who had registered with them, and when an item was bought, the shopkeeper would 'cancel' the relevant coupon in the shopper's ration book. Bacon, butter and sugar were all rationed from the start of 1940, followed by other foods we take for granted, including meat, tea, jam, biscuits and eggs.

There were two key results of this rationing – firstly, a black market in rationed foods and other goods developed, and secondly, the Dig For Victory campaign encouraged individuals to grow their own fruit and vegetables (these were not rationed, but supplies could be limited, and imports were obviously affected – bananas, for example, were nigh on impossible to obtain). Allotments around the city thrived; those without one grew what they could in their gardens and backyards. Oxford's men, women and children had, as an unexpected side-effect of these controls, a healthier lifestyle – one involving a diet limited in portion size but varied in content (and requiring a bit of imagination from wives and mothers in terms of cooking for their families), and lots of exercise. Petrol was rationed, and so walking or cycling was a logical alternative; digging in an allotment or garden provided good cardiovascular exercise and strength work.

Eating out was also affected – when restaurants were an important part of Oxford's economy. Until 1942, restaurants weren't subject to rations, which meant that Oxford's wealthier elite could supplement their diet by eating out. This was not an option for those with fewer financial resources, however, and caused resentment. When controls were placed on restaurants in the spring of 1942, although the poorer members of Oxford society might still not be able to eat out, the richer sort might not find it such an attractive option, for now, they could not have more than three courses, and only one could contain fish, game or meat. You could not have all of those within that one course – chefs could only put one of them in each dish.[33]

Rationing impacted many businesses as well as households; clothes shops were also affected, with clothes being rationed and the material used in clothes also subject to controls. But it was food rationing that had a longer term impact, one that outlasted the war itself. Poor crops after the war ended, a result of bad weather, resulted in bread rationing until 1948, and the formal rationing of food only ended in 1954. Therefore, the end of the era covered in this book saw controls on food and diet that are unimaginable to us today, with our over-consumption, fast-food restaurants and takeaways – of which, Oxford is home to many.

CHAPTER FIVE

Health

The century from 1850 saw great changes in health and mortality not just in Oxford, but across the country. Scientific and medical developments, and a growing awareness both of what caused disease and what was needed to improve people's health, improved our ancestors' lives in great measure.

One of the diseases feared by the nineteenth-century population was cholera, a disease originally thought to have been caused by 'miasma' – bad air – but that physician John Snow (1813–1858) had discovered, in 1854, to be caused by contaminated food or water, a result of poor sanitation.[1] Cholera outbreaks during the nineteenth century saw many industrial cities hit – and working-class areas were disproportionately affected. However, the dreaming spires of Oxford were not immune; there were outbreaks of cholera in the city in 1832, 1849 and 1854.[2] Two years after this final outbreak, Henry Wentworth Acland – who was appointed as Consulting Physician to the Oxford Board of Health on 6 September 1854 – produced a memoir of his experience of the 1854 epidemic.

In 1854, the Oxford Board of Health consisted of five Oxford men, including an alderman and a representative from Oriel College.[3] All cases of cholera were to be reported to them, together with cases of diarrhoea and choleraic diarrhoea, by local doctors, who would also provide a weekly return of cases.[4] These included many women, such as the 32-year-old butcher's wife – name unrecorded – from Walton Road, who died just ten hours after her symptoms started, on 6 August 1854. Cholera hit all ages – from a

16-month-old little girl, the daughter of a shoemaker, who died on Blackfriars Road on 3 September, to a 72-year-old servant's wife of Gas Street, who died the following day. In fact, women were more likely to catch cholera, but less likely to die; Henry Wentworth Acland stated that his calculations, based on the known figures, showed that 'there was a greater probability among the females that they would have the cholera; and of those who had it, there was also a greater probability that they would recover if they were males'.[5]

The figures show how those from further down the social classes – those living in more confined areas, with fewer amenities, or amenities shared with a larger number of people – were more likely to contract cholera. Labourers', carters' and travellers' wives, laundresses, needlewomen, charwomen; working-class women and those who were married to, or the daughters of, tradesmen and artisans, were listed on page after page.[6] Not all died, of course; one of the lucky ones, if you can call her that, was the unnamed 30-year-old prostitute of Shoulder of Mutton Yard in the parish of St Thomas, who recovered from the disease.[7] It was stated that there were 7.33 cases of cholera for every 1,000 people in Oxford; and 4.34 deaths. However, the figure for Oxford prison was far higher, at 47 per 1,000 cases, and 31.25 deaths. The parish of St Thomas, where the prostitute who survived cholera lived, was the worst hit parish in terms of contamination, seeing 21.81 cases of cholera per 1,000 population.[8] Henry Wentworth Acland noted that the Isis and Cherwell rivers were contaminated by the city sewers, and that sewage 'poured' into them.[9]

The latter half of the nineteenth century saw great strides being made in public health, which had the result of a 'steady decline in the Oxford death-rate', from 18.75 in 1866 to 13.00 in 1900 – the death rate in Oxford was consistently lower than the national average.[10] Yet the latter half of the nineteenth century still saw many deaths from causes that today would be survivable, with women from all backgrounds affected; however, it remained a factor that women from poorer backgrounds were more at risk of dying from certain conditions than others. Poverty brought with it the risk of death, as occurred in 1868, when a railway contractor's widow, who lived in a 'miserable room she rented in a dark court' named Wyatt's Yard, near Oxford's gaol, had no food to eat, and refused the help of the local Relieving Officer.[11] She had been persuaded at some point to enter the workhouse but, finding life 'irksome' there, she returned to her home. She got by purely on what she could pick up from the streets, and was in such a desperate plight on Christmas Day 1867 that, despite the bitter cold, she sold her two petticoats for a penny, and then spent the penny on a piece of bread to eat. Her floor was bare, and she couldn't afford to light a fire; the only piece of furniture she had was an 'old broken-backed, rickety chair'.[12] The woman, 65-year-old Martha Sargeant, was found in her hut, only partially clothed, having died of neglect and want.[13] She had apparently managed adequately while her husband, James, was alive – but when he died in 1858, his income was lost and, economically, she sank rapidly.

Martha's plight illustrated what could happen to poorer women in the days before the welfare state when their husbands, often the main income earner, died. It was only in 1942 that the Beveridge Report set out a system of welfare for all, regardless of their financial situation; and 1948, Aneurin Bevan, then the health secretary, launched the NHS.[14] But prior to this, the main option for women faced with destitution was to enter the workhouse (indeed, Martha had been sent there herself, but refused to stay). Back in 1834, the Poor Law Amendment Act had encouraged the establishment of Poor Law Unions – a group of parishes that would have their own workhouse for paupers, including orphaned children. As mentioned earlier, the city of Oxford did not want to establish a Poor Law Union, and so it was left to three unincorporated parishes – St John the Baptist, St Giles and St Clements – to join with Headington to create a new Headington Poor Law Union; Oxford continued as a separate 'incorporation' until 1926.[15] The Headington workhouse was built in the late 1830s on London Road, and initially designed to accommodate 250 people.[16] However, it was only in 1861 that a site was bought from Pembroke and Magdalen colleges on the Cowley Road, to house the new Oxford workhouse, which duly opened In 1865.

This had separate rooms for 'old men and women' and married couples, and an infirmary with wards for 'sick', convalescents, and those suffering from venereal diseases.[17] During the First World War, the workhouse became a hospital treating and rehabilitating wounded servicemen, and the workhouse inmates were sent to other places locally. It was again requisitioned and used as a hospital during the Second World War.[18]

Back in 1881, the census for the Oxford Union Workhouse showed that several elderly women were resident there; these included 72-year-old Betty Adams, who was described as an 'imbecile', 80-year-old Martha Bowles; Mary Adams, aged 76, a domestic servant, and Martha Barton, a 68-year-old dressmaker. Of course, it wasn't just older women who were at risk of becoming a pauper, as the presence of the likes of 36-year-old servant Mary Ann Bourton and 33-year-old tailoress Mary Ann Dell attest; many women, particularly those who were unmarried or widowed and entirely dependent on what they could earn on their own, were vulnerable. Many of the women in the workhouse in 1881 were servants or charwomen, laundresses or those using their needle to make a living. Piece-work, fitting in work around domestic and childcare responsibilities, or trying to work when physically incapacitated: it was easy for women to be tipped over the edge from just-about-managing to destitution.[19]

There were sanitary improvements and improved living standards in the city; a drainage scheme in the 1870s further improved the situation, as did the provision of pure water. With the former, the scheme had been planned since at least the early 1850s, with it stemming from one simple question: 'how could they get rid of their sewage?'[20] The scheme took years of planning, and vast amounts of money. The Oxford Local Board of health applied to the Local Government Board in 1875 for a loan of £100,000 to complete an ambitious sewage works scheme – following a prior loan of £40,000. These large sums were necessary for the plan involved building brick sewers, a pumping-house, boilers and pumps, as well as compensating landowners for the compulsory purchase of land, and irrigating it.[21] The system was vital, however, in improving Oxford residents' health, reducing the chances of getting such diseases as cholera or typhoid.

In terms of birth control, abstinence was seen as the well brought-up girl's correct response. Sex outside of marriage was frowned on by the press and authorities, but especially for girls. Men, conversely, could get away with 'sowing their oats' before settling down; and there was an element of acceptance to men having an affair. As is often the case with Victorian history, however, fact isn't necessarily the same as fiction. Although the Victorians have gone down in history as prudes, they were certainly not – and they were also rather sensible and practical about sex. It was not unusual for people to have sex outside of marriage, as the number of swift births following marriage attest. Accidents happened, as can be witnessed by the number of bastardy cases that came before the petty sessions courts, where the primary concern was in getting the putative father of an illegitimate child to take financial responsibility for it, rather than getting the parish involved. And by the end of the nineteenth century, Oxford's husbands would have been reading about 'the most marvellous discovery of the century' – a new line of condoms, albeit described as 'French letters', or even 'Malthusian appliances', a result of Thomas Malthus's pleas the previous century to restrict the population.[22] These were marketed to 'married men', but many a single man would have been encouraged to play the spouse and request his goods in their plain packaging. Sex was already being marketed, with the availability, by the late Victorian era, of cards featuring photographs of – to that era – scantily clad women to titillate the men.

By 1919, the late eighteenth-century John Radcliffe Infirmary was struggling with overcrowding, and had been asked to provide accommodation for those with tuberculosis. This could not be done within its existing site, and so a public appeal for funding was launched and with this, and further funding from the British Red Cross, an estate at Headington was purchased. It was here that a new Radcliffe Infirmary would be built, with separate wards for men, women and children. In 1922, a new School of Nursing opened on the new site – the first part of the hospital to be opened there.[23]

Finances were tight, though, and part of the site was sold off in the 1930s, although the hospital survived. It was only in 1931 that a maternity unit for the city's women was finished at the Radcliffe Infirmary, and this was opened in March by the Duchess of York, Elizabeth, later the Queen Mother.[24] Many women successfully gave birth there, but there were problematic labours and births as well which highlighted the issue of maternal health. June 1936, for example, saw the deaths first of one baby born at the Radcliffe – little William George Ramm – followed, two days later, by his mother, Rose Ramm (née Baker).[25] In 1941, there was a tragic incident when Annie Beutel, a 29-year-old German refugee whose husband was a German Jew interred in Australia, died. She had been admitted to the Radcliffe's Maternity Home on New Year's Day and given ether because of her 'extreme restlessness' and 'shock' of being in labour. Annie had a seizure, stopped breathing and died; she was found to have pre-eclampsia, which caused heart failure. One of the obstetrical surgeons at the Radcliffe at that time was Dr Susanna Holliday, who gave evidence at Annie Beutel's inquest.[26]

Not everyone was from as far afield as Annie Beutel, but women did come to give birth in Oxford from the surrounding areas; women such as Lily Burch, from Butlers Cross in Buckinghamshire, for example, who gave birth to a son at the Radcliffe Maternity Home in December 1931.[27] Nurses who would have helped the likes of Lily Burch included Janet Mary Reeks. Originally from Lincolnshire, she spent three years as a grammar school teacher before undertaking three years of nursing training at University College Hospital in London. She then became an SRN in October 1933, and then started work at the Radcliffe Maternity Hospital. In June 1934, she passed her Central Midwives Board examination – becoming a midwife when still only 23 years old.[28]

From physical health to mental health, and the latter was not well understood until fairly recent times. In the early nineteenth century, the parish was responsible for looking after the mentally ill, and they were often kept in the local parish workhouse; from 1845, with the passing of the Lunacy Act, county magistrates had to provide a suitable place for those paupers who had mental health issues. In Oxfordshire, 1846 saw the opening of a public asylum at Littlemore, which was gradually extended over the rest of the century. The Littlemore asylum, however, didn't only house those from the city, but also the mentally ill from Berkshire, as the city received payments from other areas for looking after their patients. Although this money was welcomed by Oxford, it resulted in overcrowding at Littlemore, and so some Oxfordshire patients found themselves sent elsewhere in return, even as far afield as London.[29] One local woman who found herself in the Littlemore Asylum was a 73-year-old lady recorded in the 1891 census as 'M.A.A.' (institutions often had their patients recorded in the census by their initials). She was a former domestic servant, described as a 'lunatic' – as was common at the time, the patients were referred to as either lunatic, imbecile, or idiot. 'A.S.', another patient, aged 20, had been sent to Littlemore from Windsor, and was described as a 'dumb idiot'. These female patients in 1891 were from largely working-class or lower-middle class backgrounds; they had worked as servants and maids, needlewomen, dressmakers, laundresses, cooks, barmaids, lace makers, glove makers, and machinists in the outside world. Few were married; most were either single or widowed.

Those who were suffering from what we would term post-natal depression or other temporary or long-term mental health issues, might also be sent there – if they were not given care within their own homes, perhaps with some dubious medicine to calm them down. Treatment given in hospitals and asylums included padded cells, restraints, and solitary confinement, although physical punishments were not allowed; this was, though, an improvement on the previous century, when manacles and chains would have kept the 'insane' close to walls, restricting their movements and granting them little humanity. However, throughout the nineteenth century, little differentiation was made between those with serious mental illnesses – including schizophrenia – and those with learning difficulties, and so they could be found housed together in an asylum in a one-size-fits-all approach, together with those suffering from depression, or 'hysteria', as females suffering from depression were often described as having.[30] Having a mental health issue was stigmatising both to the individual and their family members, and so being hidden from view in a private asylum might be the choice of an individual's family, if they had the money to pay for it; and the poorer members of society could be housed in the county asylum. Like with Oxford gaol, and the workhouse, there were few home comforts in public institutions: draughts, cold and a lack of running water might affect the patients physically as well as mentally, although conditions improved as the century progressed.

It is not surprising to find several cases of suicide in the city; suicide was a criminal offence until the passing of the 1961 Suicide Act, but depression – and the lack of understanding about it and adequate treatment of it – could lead to death.[31] In 1894, for example, 21-year-old Kate Bennett, originally from Banbury but who was lodging with her friend Mary Ann Harris at 6 Howard Street, off the Iffley Road, killed herself by drinking carbolic acid. Kate had been engaged, but her fiancé had tragically died a few weeks earlier.[32] Unsurprisingly, in the depths of grief, she was profoundly depressed, and took a drastic step to stop her pain. She left a letter to Mary Ann, asking her forgiveness and saying she 'could not bear it any more', but that her 'poor Jack' – her fiancé, John Rostron – was 'all I had to live for'. Kate had purchased the carbolic acid from a High Street chemist, Henry G. Varney, saying she needed to disinfect a drain; it wasn't one of the acids that required the purchaser to sign a register under the terms of the Sales of Poisons Act, and so Kate was free to buy and take it, with no further questions asked. At the subsequent inquest into her death, it was found that she had committed suicide 'while temporarily insane'.[33]

Four decades after Kate's death, the body of another woman – 47-year-old tailoress Ethel Hambidge – was found in the cellar of her house in Adelaide Street. She had been missing for a month. Her younger brother, Herbert Hambidge, said that she had suffered from depression and had previously had a nervous breakdown. She had also had delusions, believing the police were after her, and in the grip of these delusions, horribly, she managed to strangle herself with a length of cotton, while sitting on the floor of the cellar. She was deemed to have killed herself while her mind was disturbed.[34] In Kate's case, there was little help for her in terms of grief counselling or medical aid, despite her clear devastation at the loss of her fiancé. By the time of Ethel's death, however, there was better understanding of mental health issues, and she was seeing a doctor regularly – but this help was still not enough to prevent her tragic end.

The century from 1850 saw great changes in terms of both public health and the treatment of mental and physical health. By 1950, Oxford would be a modern city with a modern hospital, maternity facilities, and a greater understanding of the help needed for those suffering from depression, for example. Yet in some ways it was still old-fashioned, as was the nation as a whole, with suicide still seen as a crime, aberrant behaviour. In addition, the gender-specific issues facing women, such as death in childbed, or the effect of poverty or of the loss of a spouse or parent on one's economic survival as well as physical, still existed, as they had done a century earlier.

CHAPTER SIX

Leisure

In 1912, the Bishop of Oxford gave a sermon to female workers in the city, and bemoaned the fact that 'people content to spend their lives in the pursuit of amusement, living on the labour of others, were as much outside the rudiments of the covenant of God as if they denied the Christian creed'.[1] Given that he was addressing working women when he made the comment, it appears that it was, by this time, acceptable for women to be occupied in gainful employment – but not to be ladies of leisure, seeking entertainment rather than employment. Yet, as the nineteenth century progressed, the rise in consumerism and in theatrical entertainments, for example, meant that there were more and more ways for both men and women to entertain themselves in leisure activities.

Shopping for the home was largely undertaken by women, and they had plenty of choice in Oxford. Some shops explicitly advertised their services to women; in 1877, for example, the company of Charles Badcock, at 12-13 Queen Street, placed an advert in the *Oxford Times* to 'the ladies of Oxford', stating:

> Madam, the time having now arrived when it is usual for me to call your special attention to a choice selection of goods suitable for the season, and owing to the late depression of trade, I have been able to secure a large variety of novelties in each department on very advantageous terms... I am, Madam, your obedient servant, Charles Badcock.[2]

Badcock was also selling black and coloured silks, Welsh flannel, Witney blankets, 'plain and fancy hose in every size', kid gloves, silk scarves, fur muffs, mantles and jackets – as well as more practical sealskin jackets, ulsters and waterproof coats. It's clear that if money was not a problem, there was something for everyone in Oxford – and that women were marketed to by local businesses keen to get their custom. This female-oriented advertising was not new; in 1862, Belinda Searle, a milliner based at 3 Beaumont Street, had 'begged to inform the Ladies of Oxford' that her showrooms featured 'every novelty in Parisian millinery', adding the note, 'Wedding and Mourning orders on the shortest season'.[3] Nearly half a century later, in 1910, marketing hadn't changed much: Fridette's French Hat Shop at 20 George Street ('adjoining New Theatre!') was still advertising French-style hats for women wanting new clothes for the winter, but the styles had changed to reflect the times – Fridette's was also advertising its 'dainty designs in motor millinery'.[4]

Although many shops have come and gone over the decades, some remain familiar to us today, particularly Boswell's, which since 1929 has been on a site on Broad Street. Boswell's originated back in the 1730s, with Francis Boswell selling travel goods; by the 1880s, one of its neighbours was the Oxford Drug Company, and in 1890, Arthur Pearson, its owner, took over Boswell's as well. The Oxford Drug Company, during the Edwardian era, had two branches in the city – at 1 Broad Street, and 132 High Street, having bought the former May's Drug Stores at the latter location – with Boswell's being based around the corner at 49 and 50 Cornmarket Street.[5]

Boswell's emphasised its usefulness to women, advertising, in 1908, its range of 'ladies' vanity and purse bags, dressing and jewel cases, purses', and advising potential customers to 'see windows' for examples of its merchandise.[6] The Oxford Drug Company, in turn, highlighted its provision of 'perfumes in fancy cases and bottles, eau de cologne, hair brushes, etc'.[7] Window displays were part of the shopping experience, enabling both serious shoppers and browsers – as well as those who had little money to spend but who wanted to dream about potential purchases – the chance to window shop, to have their eye caught by something particularly attractive.

Christmas was a key period for both shop owners and shoppers; the Oxford Drug Company marketed its perfumes as 'choice Xmas perfumes' while the Educational Supply store at 8 Queen Street marketed its Christmas cards and calendars, and Thomas Witcomb, a watchmaker and jeweller at 4 New Inn Hall Street, was in 1901 stressing that its silver and rolled gold brooches were perfect 'for Christmas presents and New Year gifts.[8] By the 1920s, Boswell's had become associated as hardware merchants, but also sold kitchen equipment, cutlery and household linen.[9] At the same time, shopping was becoming full-scale entertainment, and for a week in September 1923, the Oxford Shopping Carnival was held, featuring 'enormous attractions, competitions, free gifts, grand carnival procession, fete and fireworks', all aimed, of course, at getting people into the city centre's shops. There was even a souvenir handbook, to make women feel that they were part of a really special event, rather than being encouraged to come in and spend money.[10]

What did women do apart from shop, when they were looking for a leisure activity? For those who could afford it, they may have visited the theatre. Like many British cities, Oxford has had a long history of theatre-going, and women were a significant part of both the theatrical profession and theatre audiences. The primary theatre was the Victoria, which had opened off Magdalen Street in 1836. By law, no plays could be performed there during university terms, so concerts and music hall productions took place then instead. The theatre became gradually more dilapidated, and in the 1880s, the decision was made to replace it. Therefore, the New Theatre on George Street opened in February 1886, designed to seat around 900 people. It must have been an impressive sight for initial audiences, being lit by a sun burner, and with the stalls seats covered in red velvet. The first performance at the theatre was by the Oxford University Dramatic Society, who performed *Twelfth Night*.[11] Of course, at this time, the dramatic society was composed largely of men, but women associated with the university did take on the roles of Olivia, Viola, and Maria – Olivia, for example, was played by a Miss Farmer. It continued to put on plays and concerts despite a fire damaging it in 1892; and in 1908, it was enlarged, to cater for an audience of up to 1,200.[12]

The New Theatre joined other places of entertainment in the city, such as the Lyric Hall, which opened on the Cowley Road in 1898; in that year, Mademoiselle Patrice, whose company was performing at the Lyric, was involved in a car accident. She was returning to her lodgings after the Friday night performance with several others – including another member of her company, Alice Winifred – when the front wheel of the car became caught in the groove of the tram line. The car 'collapsed' as it tried to turn around, and the passengers were thrown into the road. Mademoiselle Patrice was able to continue with her performance the next evening, having only been shaken, but Alice Winifred was absent, due to a dislocated shoulder.[13]

The Theatre Royal was the key Oxford theatre in the nineteenth century; as previously stated, no theatres were allowed to put on plays during university terms, and so the Theatre Royal was originally designed to be a temporary theatre that operated during the summer break.[14] Former naval officer turned actor and theatre proprietor Edward Hooper – known as 'Gentleman Ned' for his courteousness – first got permission for this in 1857, when he had a theatre built on an existing tennis court, and opened on 3 August with a performance from London theatre actors.[15][16] Two years later, he leased the Star Assembly Room, which was converted into a theatre; the first production here was performed again by actors taken from the main London theatres, as well as from theatres in Dublin and Birmingham.[17] The theatre continued every summer until 1864, when Hooper decided to stop – perhaps due to ill-health as he died soon after, of bronchitis.[18]

There was now a scrabble for 'ownership' of theatre performances, with toyshop owner Mr Adams requesting a licence. However, his competition was none other than Edward Hooper's widow, who had been left without an income, but who had the experience gained from working unofficially with her husband. Elizabeth Hooper was, like her husband, a former actor, both having been with the Theatre Royal, Drury Lane, in the late 1830s and the Theatre Royal in Brighton in the mid 1840s. As Elizabeth Ann Glover, she had married Edward – whose real name was Edward Cooper Pulliblank – at St Giles in the Fields in London on 26 September 1809, when she was around 18 years old.[19] They had known some of the great actors of the day, such as Charles Kemble and Madame Vestris, and both had a wealth of experience of the theatrical profession.[20]

Despite being too grief-stricken to argue her case before the magistrates herself – licences requiring approval by them – and having to employ a family friend, a journalist – Joseph Plowman – from the *Oxford Times*, to appear on her behalf, Mrs Hooper's experience won out and she was granted the licence from 31 July 1865. She had significant public support, and appreciated it; on 8 July, she placed a notice in the *Oxford Chronicle*, to 'tender her best thanks to the authorities for their great kindness in placing her in the proud position so lately, and for many years held by her late lamented husband. She feels it the greatest honour that can be paid to his memory.'[21]

Her season opened at the town hall, which she had had 'fitted up in a very commodious manner', and she had secured an orchestra conducted by J. F. Fielder of London's Royal Princess' Theatre, to give her theatre a touch more class. Her first play was the comedy *London Assurance*, and she had employed two actors from the Theatre Royal, Drury Lane, and another – comedian G.K. Maskell – from the Lyceum, also in London, who was making his first ever appearance in Oxford. This was followed by the farce *The Widow's Victim*, which had been played in Oxford before, but which was received well by audiences. Actress Miss Hudspeth, described as 'so great a favourite here a few seasons ago' appeared again, and was enthusiastically received.[22] G. K. Maskell played not one but three characters in the farce, and he and Miss Hudspeth's scenes together 'provoked roars of laughter'.[23]

Despite her popularity in Oxford, and the success of these first productions, Mrs Hooper only had one season in charge of the Theatre

Royal in Oxford. In October 1865, she noted that it was 'positively the last six nights' of performances at the Theatre Royal, Town Hall, still proudly noting that it was 'under the sole management of Mrs Hooper, widow of the late Mr Edward Hooper'.[24] In this final week of performances, there was 'dancing each evening by the Misses Taylor'. By 1866, Mrs Hooper was leasing the Theatre Royal in Cambridge.[25] The same year, the Oxford magistrates refused to grant a theatrical licence for that summer, leading to an aggrieved letter to the *Oxford Chronicle* from William Ogden of 4 Holywell Street that argued there was no reason to reject a licence as 'no charge of impropriety of any kind appears to have been brought against either of Mrs Hooper or her audiences', and that therefore the magistrate's decision was a 'gratuitous insult' to her. Another letter writer, builder Joseph Curtis, of 26 Pembroke Street, noted that 'one hundred of a thousand of the population of Oxford patronise[d] Mrs Hooper and the theatre', although this writer recognised that some had made the argument that audiences would have been larger had admission rates been lower, thus opening the theatre up to the average 'working man'.[26]

In 1882, two of the Theatre Royal's current actresses were advertising their engagements there – Elise Grey, who had been playing Viola, Desdemona, Leah, and Lady Teasle 'every evening', and Nellie Grey, who specialised in playing juveniles and performing in comedies and burlesques. The *Oxford Guardian* had described Nellie as being 'certainly an acquisition to the Oxford boards, her appearance being most attractive, while her abilities, judging from what we have seen, are evidently of a high order.'[27]

Although one needed some money to go to the theatre, as nothing was free, it would be a fallacy to assume that it was only open to the wealthy. In fact, all classes could enjoy the theatre – there was an establishment and a ticket for everyone. In 1896, for example, admission prices at the New Theatre varied from sixpence for the gallery to five shillings for a seat in the stalls. The dress circle cost four shillings, and the pit two shillings.[28] The New Theatre in the late 1890s saw the D'Oyly Carte opera company perform *The Mikado*, and put on an annual pantomime (in January 1895,

The Forty Thieves – described as 'Mr Milton Bode's gorgeous pantomime' – was being performed).[29]

Meanwhile, in 1900, the struggling Lyric Hall – which had previously been known as the Constitutional Hall – became The Empire Theatre of Varieties, describing itself as 'the most comfortable and attractive place of entertainment in the provinces'.[30] It offered a more eclectic range of entertainment, from the American Mystifiers, who could 'out-do spiritualists' with their performances, to Signor Pepi, 'Italy's greatest quick-change artist'.[31] In February 1900, Miss Daisy Deroy's Grande Company was performing, followed the next week by Harry B. Monkhouse and his 'company of star artistes'. The Empire was proud of its rapidly changing programme, boasting that it had an 'entire change of artistes each week'.[32] The New Theatre was, by 1909, mimicking the type of programme offered by the Empire, publicising appearances by the likes of ventriloquist Fred Russell, banjoists Emil and Ediss, and conjuror Henri Bekker.[33] Meanwhile, the East Oxford Theatre was, in 1907, also offering a variety show that included songs from Ethel Gale and dancing from the Sisters Pritchard. Another of its shows included 'A Warning to Women'![34]

Variety continued to be popular with Oxford audiences well into the twentieth century; in 1941, the New Theatre's variety performances were still attracting large audiences, despite the omnipresence of war, with female performers including The Six Melody Maids. This sextet of singers were described as 'beautifully groomed and dressed, and pleasant to the ear'. They sang a medley of popular songs, ballads and Strauss, and featured Sylvia Handel, who was remembered for her broadcast entitled From Opera to Jazz. They shared the programme with the likes of Michael Arnaud and Peggy, a pair of tap-dancing acrobats.[35] At the end of the Second World War, in 1945, the New Theatre was still offering 'humour and comedy, scintillating with artistic spectacle and alluring singing', with 'novelty presented in three renowned acts'.[36]

By this time, the New Theatre had been joined by the Oxford Playhouse, which opened as a repertory theatre in 1938. Fundraising for this theatre had started back in 1934, with the aim of raising

£25,000. Although there was local opposition to the plans, the design soothed many, and it was duly built on land leased by St John's College, at Beaumont Street. It had a resident company of actors performing one play every evening, while spending the days rehearsing the next play. The first play, James B. Fagan's *And So To Bed*, opened on 20 October 1938.[37]

At the other end of the scale, the Oxford University Musical Club was, at the same time, performing classical concerts at the town hall which were open to the general public. In March 1898, one such concert comprised string quartets by Hayden, Brahms and Beethoven, performed by the Berlin Quartet.[38] If a lady wished to play an instrument herself – and playing the piano, for example, was seen as a very desirable skill for an educated lady in Victorian times – she could visit James Russell and Co's warehouse at 120 High Street, where Bechstein pianos, American organs and harmoniums could be bought. Cash discounts were offered, but the instruments could also be hired by the day, week, month, year or even for three years – a form of our hire-purchase.[39] James Russell's had been a thriving concern since at least the 1860s, when it was also an agent for Theatre Royal tickets and season tickets.[40]

Such formal entertainment might be out of the financial reach of some women, or they might prefer more informal events. For these women, musical entertainments put on in their own homes, with 'repasts' (dinners or teas) were popular.[41] Other repasts were part of political or social causes which Oxford women were members of (more details of which can be found later in this book), such as a 'tea and entertainment' evening held at Oxford Town Hall in 1893, which was linked to the Liberal Unionists and the Primrose League. The tea, which 300 attended, was organised by several notable women, such as Georgina Müller – the wife of philologist (Friedrich) Max Müller, and a woman who had been active in supporting education for women and the Oxford High School for Girls – and the Honourable Edith Lyttelton Gell, whose husband Philip was an editor at the Oxford University Press. As with many of these teas or other events put on in the city, the same names appear time and time again in the local newspapers in terms of organising, or helping, with the events. The wives of Oxford academics, politicians, or other movers and shakers in the city would regularly help their husbands with their events by taking on organisational roles, or helping with entertainment or other events. In the days before women could take on a political role in their own right, such involvement demonstrated a desire to help society on a local or national scale, as well as to be 'helpful' and support their spouses, fathers, or male siblings, and to socialise with other women from their own, or similar, backgrounds.[42]

For those wishing to develop their skills at public speaking, there was a Church Society for Training The Speaking Voice, which held meetings at 21 St Michael's Street. At the turn of the twentieth century, Caroline D'Orsey, the society's honorary secretary and lecturer in elocution at King's College London, was giving lectures on physical voice training, arguing that to train one's voice prevented the individual from getting throat disease, and had also published a book entitled *Cultivation of the Speaking Voice*. The society also employed Cyril Streatfeild, himself a singer as well as being a professor at Trinity College London, to give singing and intonation lessons.[43]

This gives an indication both of how much there was to do in Oxford, and how women could take advantage of the increasing number of options for entertainment and consumerism as the nineteenth century turned into the twentieth. But it was not all mindless entertainment; in fact, even consumerism and shopping could be a political experience. In 1881, a hint of this was given in a Banbury newspaper, where Lady Harberton's Dress Reform Association was discussed. This association aimed to get women wearing bloomers instead of petticoats; the newspaper noted: 'The difference in the general appearance of a lady who wears a petticoat on each leg instead of enclosing the two in one, and covering them up with a tunic, or skirt, is so slight that masculine criticism is quite disarmed.'[44]

The campaign for bloomers had started in the US in the 1850s. Reformers included Harriet Austin, Lydia Sayer Hasbrouck, Mary Walker and Ellen Beard Harman, all of whom had medical degrees.

Women 'adopted Bloomers to better their health ... Wisconsin women contributed reports on difficulties with their husbands accepting the Bloomer and wearing the Bloomer for farmwork. A physician wore hers on her rounds to visit patients...'[45] Back in 1858, *Reynolds's Newspaper* copied a comment from the New York Times:

> From crinoline to pants is a vast collapse. Yet there are women who covet the change. We have before us a paper called The Sibyl, published at Middletown, New York, which purports to be 'devoted to dress reform'. Its head bears, as a pictorial embellishment, the figure of a woman in the full Bloomer costume. There she stands...with petticoats reaching no lower than her knees. There is no expansion of hoops, the drapery falling around the form without the slightest attempt at the dimensions of a balloon. The Sibyl is the organ of the 'National Dress Reform Association', a body which holds conventions, makes speeches, reads letters, and publishes resolutions in the most approved style of latter-day progress. Politicians, clergymen, and grave professors lend their influence in favour of the pantaloons propaganda, and assure the breeches-loving women of their profoundest sympathy.[46]

In 1866, a Scottish newspaper reported on the Women's Dress Reform Convention that was being held at Syracuse. It noted that 'in the United States there is a society called the National Dress Reform Association' that organised the convention, and its president, Dr Mary E. Walker of Oswego, had suggested changing the organisation's name to the National Dress Reform and Equal Rights Association, illustrating how women's desire to dress practically was aligned to being given the same rights as men to dress how they wanted, and in a way that suited their lives.[47]

Bloomers had already reached Britain by this point; in 1851, the *Reading Mercury* had eagerly headlined one story, 'First appearance of the Bloomer costume in London', which reported that two ladies – a Mrs Jeffers, 37, and her 18-year-old daughter – had been seen walking down Oxford Street on a Saturday afternoon, 'attired in the Bloomer costume and escorted by a crowd of ragged urchins, and a number of the curious of both sexes'.[48] It was made clear that the Jeffers women were rather alternative anyway – for they had 'recently arrived in the metropolis to attend the vegetarian soiree'. They wore pink-striped 'pantaloons', which attracted so much 'troublesome' attention that the women had to leap into a cab to escape – something they were able to speedily do, thanks to their practical clothing.

That autumn, the *Oxford Chronicle* reported the 'advent of Bloomerism in Abingdon', when a lecture was held on the subject in the council chamber, attended by a large number of women. The men in the audience, however, disrupted the talk so much that the female speaker had to finish early. She was detailed by the paper as wearing black satin: 'she wore a straw coloured silk hat with a lace fall; a cloak, fastened at the throat, and which reached to the knees, below which the ample trowsers [*sic*] were seen, and these terminated at the ankle, where they were tied; a pair of boots, edged with fur, completed her costume. Her demeanour was characterised with great modesty, but her appearance was not attractive.'[49] As was usually the case, the female was judged not on what she did, but on how attractive she looked. In 1899, a women's column in the *Oxford Journal*, written by a local woman, noted that,

> no sensible woman dresses to please men; she makes men like what she chooses to wear. I don't believe men have any objection to bloomers. A man objects to his own women folk doing anything to attract attention, but if only other men's wives, sisters, cousins, and aunts wore bloomers for cycling he would jump at the chance of graciously permitting his own belongings to do the same.'[50]

As cycling became a more popular activity, it was inevitable that women would increasingly demand to wear practical clothing, including bloomers. Three women set off on their bicycles from Hyde Park Corner in September 1897, aiming to cycle to Oxford. It was noted that the 'enormous crowd' present to see them off had 'braved the bitterly-cold wind and rain to see the lady cyclist in rational costume, and were determined to have some fun.' Men, women and children all stared at these women 'as though they were natural curiosities, and ventilated their wit upon the bloomers. It is only just to say that so neat and workmanlike were the ladies' costumes that even the British matron could not have brought a complaint against the wearers on the score of impropriety.'[51]

It was also, perhaps, inevitable that the wearing of bloomers would be so controversial. They challenged the patriarchal perceptions of femininity, with women wearing items of dress for purely practical, rather than decorative, purposes. This was not about them looking attractive for their men, but about making themselves feel comfortable and enabling them to undertake activities such as cycling without worrying about their dresses getting in the way or getting damaged. They increased women's sense of independence, and this was a threat to the status quo and to concepts not only of femininity but of masculinity as well.

For a long period, the wearing of bloomers continued to be 'niche', with those trend-setters who wore them being teased, debated, and mocked, as can be seen from the examples detailed here. But most women in Oxford continued as they always had; those who could afford to keep up with fashion would read the fashion pages of the local and national press to find out what was 'in', and where they could buy such items. In 1866, for example, Oxford women were told that 'chinchilla fur is again in', and should be used for trimming dresses or tunics. Muffs and boots could also be trimmed with this fur; but on coats (paletots), only the collar and reverses of sleeves should be trimmed. White tulle ball-dresses were fashionable; young women could wear dresses embroidered with daisies, and bonnets should be 'delicate' and made of black velvet and lace.[52]

Women read about these latest fashions in the newspapers, and the stores of Oxford also grabbed their attention with their large adverts in the same publications. John Juggins, with two city centre stores, at Magdalen Street and George Street, advertised his show of mantles and millinery for the latest 'season'; Edward Beaumont, based at 9 High Street, stressed that his selection of mantles were 'large, cheap and beautiful', while separately assuring his female customers that his own elastic bodice and expanding self-lacing stays would 'avoid tight lacing'.[53] H. Baker and Co, on Castle Street, appealed to local women's desire to dress like the rich and famous by stating that its own fast-pile velveteen was admired by the likes of actresses Sarah Bernhardt and Madge Kendal.[54] In the 1870s, Queen Street's Charles Badcock – mentioned before – sent an advert, in the form of a formal letter, to 'the ladies of Oxford', boasting of his success in making 'purchases in the best English and Foreign markets', and his subsequent 'first show of New Goods for the coming season'.[55] But by the fin de siècle, practicality was taking a more prominent place – and ladies' waterproofs, for example, were being sold at J. Zacharias & Co at 26-27 Cornmarket Street.[56]

CHAPTER SEVEN

Prison Life

Oxford's medieval prison had been replaced by a new one in the late eighteenth century, and by the start of the nineteenth it housed over 100 prisoners, divided into male and female wings. In the late 1840s and early 1850s, it was further expanded, housing double the previous number of inmates. The majority of prisoners were male – by 1856, over 200 of the imprisoned felons were male compared to women who numbered only in the twenties; the debtors, also housed in the prison, were over 100 men but again only around twenty-five women.[1] This was not unusual, by any stretch, for women tended to commit fewer crimes, or serious crimes, than men, and there tended to be more leniency shown towards female offenders than male. Where women committed crimes, they were more likely to commit verbal or minor physical assaults that could be dealt with at a community level, or at petty sessions, and be punishable with a warning, the binding over to good behaviour, or a fine. Theft was an offence committed both by men and women, with the latter often stealing items of dress, or small items related to dressmaking, from local shops. In 1856, for example, three women were charged with stealing nine mantles and a length of ribbon from the shop of William Boleman at 9 High Street; they had asked Mr Boleman for bonnets, and while he was looking for someone, stole the other goods. Two of the women, Corty and Roberts, were serial offenders; they had also stolen five baby robes, another five mantles, and five parasols, from William Guy at 47 Cornmarket Street – and passed some of the goods onto Smith to sell. Again, the two women had asked William Guy for bonnets, and his assistant sent them into the shop's showroom. The assistant then went out to get more products, leaving the women alone – and after they had gone, it was found that some of the goods were missing. Two other women, Emma Gilkes and Sarah Green, gave evidence against the accused females.[2]

Oxford had its own Female Penitentiary and House of Refuge, aimed at rescuing fallen women – described in a newspaper of 1862 as 'this excellent institution'.[3] Yet residents didn't know much about it; indeed, in 1854, it was noted that 'it may to very many be unknown'.[4] When plans had been put into motion to establish it back in the early 1830s, it was noted that it would be 'the only institution in Oxford for the present improvement and reformation leading to the eternal happiness of an unfortunate and numerous class of females'.[5] The Penitentiary aimed at the outset to prevent fallen women from either becoming prostitutes or committing suicide – this being, of course, a criminal offence at the time. In Oxford, the unfortunate women who the Penitentiary aimed to help were divided into two classes:

> The one, those who are seduced from places of service; the other, children of Oxford parents, who associate with and live near to the prostitutes: of the latter class, nearly all enter into the path of ruin before they are seventeen years of age, very many before they are sixteen, and some as young as fourteen years of age.[6]

Prior to the Penitentiary opening, the only recourse of the authorities for women in trouble was to incarcerate them within the city gaol; but this was not ideal, for here, the young were housed with 'prostitutes or felons ... hardened and old offenders', who treated the fallen girl with derision.[7] However, other girls deemed to have been marginalised from nineteenth century society – thieves, those suffering from alcoholism, and the homeless.

The penitentiary opened in 1833, being housed originally in premises on Brewer Street in the city centre. This central location, though, had a problem – it was too near temptation. There were pubs and taverns, alleys where prostitutes plied their trade. In addition, the building was poorly maintained, and inadequate for its purposes. In south Oxfordshire, the St Mary's Home in Wantage was being held up as an example of how women should be housed and treated; it opened in 1850, and received a regular number of women, who were regarded as having then made a 'successful' reintroduction into ordinary life. In 1854, it was decided to send a fixed number of women from the Oxford Female Penitentiary to St Mary's, for a sum of £100 a year. This was seen as a temporary measure, however, with there being a clear need to keep the Oxford building running, but at the same time helping St Mary's to expand its own buildings.[8] In 1857, the Penitentiary finally moved to a different location – the Holywell Manor House, next to St Cross Church, in a quieter part of the city.

Now, the penitentiary came under the aegis of the Community of St John the Baptist, a religious order founded in 1852, which had a convent at Clewer, near Windsor in Berkshire. The main aim of the community's Sisters of Mercy was to help rescue women who were unmarried mothers, prostitutes, or destitute. They would be given a roof over their heads, food and company, and also be taught skills that could help them gain respectable jobs. The community was founded by Harriet Monsell, the widow of a clergyman, who became its first Sister Superior, and Reverend Thomas Thellusson Carter, the rector of Clewer, who would become the Oxford Female Penitentiary's warden for fifty years, until he died in 1901, aged 88.[9] At the penitentiary, a sister superior was in charge, with other members of staff (sisters of mercy) usually only being in the single figures.[10] The sisters were women who wanted to help others less fortunate than themselves; in helping others, they gained more interesting employment than might otherwise have been open to them in the nineteenth century, and also had the companionship of the other sisters, and security – as well as a sense of being part of a spiritual community.[11]

Houses of Mercy and similar female penitentiaries were usually set up and run by those from religious orders. Nuns might not seem an obvious choice for this role because of their relative unworldliness, but they believed in redemption, and that women could 'learn' morality and how to live a respectable life, without the need to control them through punishment, unlike in the traditional penal institution. However, the governors of the penitentiary were all men: the institution's regulations stated that they should be clergymen or gentlemen. The main qualification for acting as a governor was money: to be eligible, you had to have set up an annual subscription to the penitentiary, or have donated a certain sum.[12] The amount required by non-clergy was twice that of their religious acquaintances. Religion underpinned penitentiary life, with religious readings taking place, and the penitents required to mendicate and pray. They were told to repent of their sins, and to develop a 'spirit of vigilance and diligence, and a constant habit of serious prayer'.

Shortly before Reverend Carter's death, a new wing of the penitentiary was opened; it was still offering refuge for fallen women, who were then sent out to work in service, or who then moved to live with friends or in other homes, if they so wanted. In this year, the penitentiary's chaplain recorded that 'two girls who had been sent away as apparently hopeless, some two years ago' had recently communicated with him and he had been reassured by the fact that they now appeared to be 'really penitent'. As with many aspects of life in the nineteenth and early twentieth centuries, there was a clearly religious purpose to these homes; not only were they overseen by the church, but the girls' difficulties were often portrayed as having a religious aspect. In 1902, for example, one girl, who had left the penitentiary back in 1891, was noted to have since 'steadily persevered in the right way in the face of great difficulty, her employers being dissenters, and not approving of her going to church.'[13]

The penitentiary continued until 1929 and, by the twentieth century, was working with both local women and those from outside the Oxford area. The 1881 census records thirty-three female penitents in the building, all but two being from counties other than Oxfordshire. Seven of the women were Londoners, but others came from elsewhere in England as well as from Wales and Ireland. They were primarily women in their late teens, although one, Emily Pow, a Londoner, was older, at 31. The youngest penitents there in 1881 were Eliza Collier and Emily Butt, both aged 15.[14] On the 1881 census the women were recorded as 'penitents', in 1891 they were 'inmates' as though in prison; in 1901 they were listed as laundry maids, perhaps in an attempt to mask their 'unfortunate' status within late Victorian society, but also reflecting the fact that they had to do both the penitentiary's washing, as well as taking in washing from other households. This laundry work trained the girls to do a job, but it also had a religious significance – in cleaning clothes, they were also cleaning themselves of sin. Not everything was to do with 'cleansing' the women, though, and the sisters tended to rely on making women feel part of a close-knit community, learning skills together, rather than shaming them for their perceived immorality. By 1911 the census was recording them as 'boarders', a more neutral word that masked their status as inmates of a penitentiary. The ultimate goal was to send these women back out into the world, armed with practical skills that would help them earn money through legitimate means, but also, hopefully – to the sisters – with a sense of God being with them on their journey.

The censuses gives a snapshot both of the sisters in charge of the Oxford penitentiary, and those whom they looked after. In the 1880s, a sister from the Clewer convent, Dubliner Fidelia Maturin, was brought in as Sister Superior of the institution – and she stayed there for the next 20 years, before returning to Clewer. In 1891, penitents tended to be older than the earlier residents, but there were still several younger girls there, including Ada Mary Iles, from Wiltshire, who was 17, and Oxford-native Ada Haymaker, who was just 15 years old. Although some girls, like Ada, were from the city, many were not; in fact these penitents were drawn from a wide geographical area. In 1891, for example, women in the penitentiary included several from the south-west of England, and others from London, Surrey, Birmingham and Ireland. One girl, 22-year-old Annie Stringer, had been born even further away – in Florida.

As the nineteenth century progressed, the Female Penitentiary was joined by the House of Refuge, minutes away on St Aldate's. This opened in 1875, providing temporary accommodation for fallen women (the Female Penitentiary was able to house more women, for longer, than the House of Refuge). In 1899, Hope Cottage, run by the Oxford Ladies' Association, opened, providing a home for women with their babies; and a second home run by the same organisation opened at St Frideswide's in 1902. The growth of establishments in Oxford was reflected across the UK – within a few years of the beginning of the twentieth century, there were over 200 penitentiaries run by Anglican organisations or communities, whereas sixty years earlier there had only been around ten. They may have seemed in some ways, to be old-fashioned, moralistic institutions, but they continued to offer an alternative to prison or street life for many women until relatively recently. In Oxford, the Female Penitentiary continued to run at the Manor House until 1929, when it relocated to St Mary's Home in Littlemore; it then continued to operate until after the Second World War. However, times were moving on, and penitentiaries gradually became mother and child homes, before 'fallen' women finally became a more integrated part of society, regardless of their backgrounds or lifestyles.

Imagine, though, that you were not a fallen woman, but a criminal one – a woman who had behaved in a way deemed abhorrent and unnatural to her 'gentler' sex. You had committed murder. What would happen to you? Luckily, by the mid nineteenth century, the Bloody Code of the previous century – the list of some 200 offences that were capital offences – had been whittled away, and now, only a certain number of the worst crimes were punished with hanging. Luckily, the offence of petty treason, whereby a woman could be burned at the stake for killing her husband or employer (an offence not applicable to men who killed their wives, of course), had ended. However, until 1868, the remains of an earlier, less 'civilised' society were still there in part. For example, the hangings of convicted felons took place in public – in Oxford, this was on Castle Green or on a mound by Westgate.[15] From 1868, hangings had to be held in private, and this would have been done in a prison yard – although the public would still gather outside the walls and watch for a flag to be lifted to denote that the hanging had been carried out. However, from 1837 until the ending of capital punishment in the 1960s, no woman was hanged at Oxford.[16]

This does not mean that women did not commit murder; but juries were more disposed to find them guilty of lesser offences in order to avoid a judge having to pass a death sentence on them. This was the case in 1876, when Charlotte Hill and Matilda Saunders were charged at the Oxford Assizes with murdering Matilda's baby. Both women had difficult lives; Charlotte was deaf and dumb, and Matilda already had a son before having another child who was illegitimate. Despite Charlotte 'virtually admitting' having burned the baby's body in the fire – the police found charred human remains in the grate when they searched – the jury only found the two women guilty of the concealment of a birth (rather than finding Matilda guilty of infanticide), and they were sentenced to two years in prison each. At the same Assizes, Mary Ann Beck, who was married, was charged with the wilful murder of her child, but acquitted on the grounds of insanity.[17]

The 1881 census reflects this male-dominated environment behind prison walls. There are a few women listed because they were married to prison warders – such as Hannah Furze, 36, from Somerset, Sarah Lanchbury, 36, from Warwickshire; 18-year-old Emma Waters lived at the prison with her father, Nathaniel, the chief warden, and her 16-year-old brother Walter.[18] Maud Sparshott was the matron, assisted by Susanna Wetherall; neither was originally from the city, although Susanna was from Abingdon. Life in the prison could be harsh, with few home comforts; prisoners had to deal with the cold, with a strict and monotonous diet, and with bare, uncomfortable cells. For misbehaving – which included both physical actions and a 'bad' attitude – they could be sent into solitary confinement. Women would have been given jobs to do in the prison washhouse, or have helped prepare food; oakum-picking was another common, and soul-destroying task.

Even into the twentieth century, conditions in prison and a poor understanding about how to deal with prisoners could lead to injuries or death. In November 1910, for example, a 25-year-old woman named Alice Brown died in Oxford Prison. At her inquest, it was found that she had had undiluted carbolic acid applied to her head as a medicinal remedy by a member of the prison staff – who had forgotten to dilute the acid with water first. Alice ingested some of the acid, and it burned her insides, causing her kidneys and heart to fail; a doctor called to examine the body stated that 'a grievous and serious error was made' by the prison.[19]

It was more common for women to be the victims rather than the perpetrator of a serious crime; Lucy Smith, for example, was gypsy who lived with her husband Charles and children in a tent near Cowley. On 19 February 1887, Lucy's husband beat her to death with a hammer – their children were present, but were asleep and left unharmed; 63-year-old Charles Smith was hanged at Oxford three months after the murder.[20]

Lucy Smith's murder was an extreme case, but domestic violence was by no means unheard of in Oxford during the nineteenth and twentieth centuries. Although cases of such violence are relatively unreported in the Oxford press compared with some other areas, it should not be inferred that Oxford husbands rarely committed assaults on their wives, for domestic cases often took place behind closed doors and may have been resolved between couples, or with the help of family members – if at all. Where respectability and image were everything among middle-class Victorians, it took a lot of strength for a woman to bring a case against her husband in the courts; she risked gossip, negative comment, and for her marriage to be exposed to public scrutiny. It is understandable that some cases may simply not have come before the courts, and therefore not be reported in the press; many women must have simply suffered in silence or separated from their husbands without seeking other action.

Look closely, however and some cases were reported – often as the result of divorce cases brought by wives who could no longer cope with their husbands' behaviour. In 1864, Lawrence Booker was charged with 'annoying and threatening his wife with personal violence'. The case against him was considered 'very gross' and Booker was sent to prison for twelve months. It is worth remembering, though, that a husband would more often be fined for marital violence than imprisoned – and Booker was only sent to the prison because he failed to find two sureties of £25 each for him to keep the peace.[21] In the summer of 1882, 73-year-old Rachel Green appeared in the Oxford City Police Court with a badly bruised face, to state that a 90-year-old man from Great Clarendon Street, Joseph Scarsbrook, had violently assaulted her. Joseph wasn't her husband, but Rachel had been hit by him while trying to defend his wife from his drunken violence. The situation was complicated; Rachel insisted that Joseph wouldn't have been violent if he had been sober, and Joseph's defence argued that he had 'accidentally' hit Rachel while protecting himself from his wife's violence! Although Joseph was fined five shillings for assault, the case shows how women depended on their female friends and neighbours for support when their husbands were violent, and also how drink was seen both as a motivation and an excuse for violence.[22]

Women were not just the victims of violence or neglect, however – they could be the violent party themselves. In 1892, the NSPCC published a report on its work in Oxfordshire, where its Oxford Branch had been working for the previous seven months. It made clear that 'seven months have sufficed to dispel the idea that there is no cruelty in our county'. In that seven months, it had seen thirty-six cases, ten of which required prosecution (and all of which resulted in a conviction). Some of those detailed were cases brought against mothers. In one, a 'violent-tempered woman' had regularly struck and thrown things at her 12-year-old daughter, hitting her so often that the girl was left 'no better than an imbecile'.

Although the mother was prosecuted and bound over to keep the peace for a year, there was no happy ending. The parent avoided prison because she was 'a cripple'; her daughter was sent to the workhouse. A second, poverty-stricken, woman had taken to singing in the streets with her two young children, to get money. The children were used as their mother thought their appearance would get people's sympathy, and thus get her more money. She was arrested for making the children beg; but it was then found that a man – presumably, although not explicitly stated, her husband – had ordered her to go out and sing in public, and it was he who was sentenced to a week's hard labour. The NSPCC said that its experience was that 'in nine cases out of ten, a woman singing in the street with children is sent out by a man, who does no work himself, sends them out in all weathers, and often ill-treats them when unsuccessful'.[23] They noted that in another case in Oxford, an unemployed man with a fondness for drink beat his wife and threatened her until she agreed to go into the street and prostitute herself. He then spent her earnings on himself, and his wife and children were left in a starving condition. He was prosecuted, and sentenced to two months' hard labour.[24]

Infanticide was treated increasingly leniently as the nineteenth century progressed. It was a capital offence, but, as has already been seen, there was a reluctance to hang women, particularly when they might have had been suffering from what we would term post-natal depression, or had been faced with losing their jobs if it was found that they had had a baby, particularly if it was illegitimate, with the stigma that went along with that. Therefore, women were increasingly convicted of concealing the birth of their child, rather than of infanticide, or if convicted, given a punishment lesser than that of death. On 12 July 1871, a 25-year-old woman, Rachel Busby, was convicted of murdering her son at the Oxford Assizes, and sentenced to death; but her son was not a baby, but a child she had been looking after, and developed a relationship with, for four years.[25] Rachel had been cohabiting with a man named Thomas Castle, although he was not the father of her son – Edward Patrick Busby, known as Teddy. Rachel had told relatives that she was sending her son to be looked after by relatives – but police had found his body tied up in a bundle of clothes under a chest of drawers in Rachel's house. He had been drowned around a month earlier.[26]

Rachel later gave a statement, saying, 'I did it. I was drove to it by the treatment of Castle … I done it to put the poor little thing out of its misery; it was so ill-treated by Castle that it was bruised from its foot to its head.' However, although the criminal register for Rachel states that 'sentence [was] passed', her sentence was soon respited.[27] Sadly, all it appears Rachel had wanted was to marry Castle, despite his alleged abuse of her and her son, and to gain a conventional family – but he had reneged on promises to marry her, and she felt that this was because the little boy 'vexed' him. In Oxford Prison, awaiting trial, she was said to be 'in a very depressed state'.[28] Another woman who appeared at the same Assizes, Mary Ann Sutton, was also indicted for murder, but unlike Rachel, she was only convicted of the lesser offence of 'endeavouring to conceal the birth of her child' and sentenced to five months in prison.[29]

Poverty was clearly a factor in many of such cases, with husbands and wives resorting to desperate measures in order to get money. Drink was a way of blotting out the unpleasantness of life for the destitute and semi-destitute, as, perhaps, some of the violence was. The lack of understanding about, or availability of, contraception could also mean that those without any economic stability might have families they could not afford to maintain. In some cases, parents might scrape together insurance premiums, insuring the lives of their infants but doing little to keep them alive – in the hope they could claim on the insurance when they died.[31] In Oxford, one woman insured the life of her youngest child – still a baby – and had publicly said that she wished the baby would die. It was certainly emaciated by the time the NSPCC stepped in. However, because the baby survived the mother was simply 'warned' about her behaviour.[32] What kind of life that baby grew up into remains unknown.

Women were no longer sent to Oxford Prison after 1924,[33] but crime continued, and women figured both as offenders and as victims of violent crimes. One of the worst of these occurred in August 1931, when a greengrocer's widow, Annie Kempson, was found dead at home in Boundary House, St Clements.[34] She had been murdered, with several stab wounds found on her body. Mrs Kempson was 58, profoundly deaf and well liked, being an active member of the congregation of St Clement's Church. She had arranged to go to London the day before with a female friend, but when she failed to turn up at their meeting place, the friend got in touch with Mrs Kempson's brother, Charles Reynolds, who was a messenger at Jesus College. He ran round to his sister's house, and when he couldn't get an answer, notified the police. They forced their way in, and found Mrs Kempson lying on the floor of a back room, covered in rugs and cushions. She had been dead around two days.

Annie Louisa Kempson had married back in 1905, to William John Kempson, a man twenty years her senior. William had died in 1925, aged 72, leaving Annie, described in the press as 'a dear, inoffensive woman who was respected by everyone', alone. Since being widowed she had taken in a young woman as her lodger;

perhaps this was to help her feel safer, as well as for company, for her house had previously been broken into – and when her body was found, the police discovered the house to be in 'disarray'.[35] Witnesses told police about a 'scarred loiterer', a 'half mental' man who 'looked like a beggar'; the police felt that whoever murdered Annie was a 'sneak-thief', a desperate individual who had forced his way in through a back window in order to rob the house, but who had then been disturbed by the widow.[36] A commercial traveller, of no fixed abode, named Henry Daniel Seymour was soon apprehended at Brighton, brought back to Oxford, and charged with Annie's murder.[37] The 39-year-old was convicted, but appealed; his appeal was heard at the Central Criminal Court in London on 23 November 1931.[38] His counsel argued that the judge at the original trial had misdirected the jury, and that the guilty verdict 'was against the weight of evidence' – but his arguments, and the appeal, were dismissed, and his original sentence of death stood.[39] He was hanged at 8 a.m. on 10 December 1931, at Oxford Prison, before a crowd of several hundred people – including many women who had stopped on their way to work – gathering outside the jail to ensure that justice was done. A few minutes after eight, a prison warder opened the gates and posted a notice confirming that Seymour was dead. The crowd had soon dispersed, and outsiders may never have guessed what had just happened.[40]

As stated previously, crimes committed by women in the Oxford area were relatively rare – and when they occurred, they commonly involved theft or assault. Women were perceived as being more verbally violent, attacking their friends, relatives or neighbours with cruel words, but they could also hit or strike individuals. During the nineteenth century, theft might be from genuine need – such as stealing bits of coal or wood in order to heat houses and cook food – but with the rise in consumerism and shopping in the late nineteenth century, together with the presence of periodicals and newspaper columns or advertisements detailing the latest fashions, some women desired clothes or accessories they could not afford and in such cases, filching items from shops could sometimes follow.

CHAPTER EIGHT

Active Citizens

Women were active in public life in various ways throughout the nineteenth and early twentieth centuries. There was a keen desire to get involved in Oxford life, to improve people's lives while also meeting other people with similar beliefs. Even in the days before women were able to become magistrates, or hold other forms of public office, there were areas where women could feel that they were making a useful contribution to how the city lived and worked. Whether through their church, or through other organisations such as trade unions, temperance societies, women's societies or friendly societies, Oxford's women were active, motivated, and keen to make a difference.

Trade unions, the successor of the medieval guild, and also known as 'combinations', had existed since the seventeenth century although, as was the case of the Tolpuddle Martyrs in early nineteenth century Dorset shows, attempts by workers to organise themselves were not appreciated by employers or the government, who attempted to prevent such collective action. For example, two Combination Acts, in 1799 and 1800, had made any strike action illegal – but this did not stop workers from calling for better pay and conditions. The Combination Acts were repealed in the 1820s, and although high profile cases such as the Tolpuddle Martyrs – who were transported to Australia on spurious charges after their attempts to form a union for agricultural labourers – put people off forming or joining unions for a while, from the 1850s and 1860s onwards, the trade union movement started to really take off.[1]

Ada Benson, founder of the Oxford High School for Girls (public domain)

The academic Max Müller, whose wife, Georgina, was an active member of Oxford society. Both Max and Georgina had a strong philanthropic streak. (public domain)

Henry Nettleship, another Oxford academic whose wife, Matilda (nee Steel), took a strong interest in the city's life and politics. (public domain)

Sylvia Pankhurst was pelted with stones by university students when she led a suffrage rally in St Giles, Oxford, in 1912. (public domain)

Harriet Monsell, who founded the Community of St John the Baptist in Clewer, Berkshire. The Community expanded to run the Oxford Female Penitentiary. (public domain)

The former Female Penitentiary, which was housed in the Holywell Manor House. (author)

Agnes Grace Weld, former muse of Lewis Carroll and Julia Margaret Cameron, worked for the poor in Oxford. (public domain)

Above: *The entrance to Somerville College, on St Giles (author)*

Left: *St Hilda's College, situated next to Magdalen College School on Cowley Place (author)*

Above: *Lady Margaret Hall today, located at the end of Norham Gardens (author)*

Right: *Much of St Ebbes Street has been rebuilt, but here, you get some sense of its history. The modern building on the right, background, was approximately where F Cape's drapery was based (author)*

Above: *The Oxford Playhouse building on Beaumont Street (author)*

Left: *The New Theatre on George Street (author)*

Above: *Boswell's – an iconic store on Oxford's Broad Street (author)*

Right: *In 1891, Agnes Weld was living with her family at 5 Norham Gardens (pictured) – next door to the Max Müller family at number 7 (author)*

The Randolph Hotel, a major employer of Oxford's women (author)

Oxford's former prison is now an upmarket hotel (author)

Henry and Annie Rogers, photographed by Lewis Carroll in 1861. Annie would become the first woman to gain honours in an Oxford university exam (public domain)

Dame Lucy Sutherland, the former principal of Lady Margaret Hall (creative commons, from the archives of Lady Margaret Hall)

Right: *Economist William Hewins attended a meeting of the Oxford Women's Trades Society in the 1890s with his wife, Margaret (public domain)*

Below: *Sarah-Jane Cooper had an active hand in the success of the Cooper's jam factory, which is still a part of the Oxford skyline today (author)*

Above: *This image, from the summer of 1920, was from one of the many fashion magazines aimed at women, encouraging them to buy new clothes (author)*

Left: *Judges Lodgings, on St Giles, was once home to the Oxford High School for Girls (author)*

By the end of the nineteenth century, trade unions specifically for women had been established, and Oxford had its own Oxford Society of Women Working in Trades. As with many other Oxford societies at the same time, this society held its annual meetings at the Wesleyan Lecture Room on New Inn Hall Street. One such meeting, on the evening of Thursday, 10 February, 1898, was only 'moderately' attended, but it did include an address given by Miss Mena Wilson, from the London Women's Trade Union League. One of those present was Oxford teacher and historian Henry Andrew Liddell; hopefully, he also had the support and involvement of his wife Emma with the society (their own daughters, Eva and Ida, being rather too young to be involved at this point, at 9 and 8 years old).[2] Matilda Nettleship presided over this meeting; she was the widow of Henry Nettleship, professor of Latin at Corpus Christi College, who had died five years earlier.[3] It's interesting that the Wikipedia entry for Henry refers to both his son and daughter, but makes no notice of his wife – an omission that seems to hark back to Victorian times, rather than being a modern recognition that a child cannot exist without two parents. Yet Henry's wife was an active participant in Oxford life, both during and after her husband's death, as her involvement in the Oxford Society of Women Working in Trades shows – she was also re-elected as a trustee of the Women's Protective and Provident Society of women working in trades in Oxford in 1902, again the same organisation but with a slightly different recording of the name.[4]

This was also presumably the same Oxford Women's Trades Society that had had its annual meeting in the same place, on a Thursday evening, back in 1892. At this meeting, Miss Holyoake, secretary of the London Women's Trades Union League, had attended, together with economist William Hewins and his wife Margaret, and Charlotte Toynbee – the latter being the widow of historian and reformer Arnold Toynbee, and an active figure in Oxford for many years.[5] In 1892, there were seventy-nine paying members of the society, and thirty-four had needed a sick allowance during the year, together with two members needing an out-of-work payment. At this meeting, Miss Holyoake had given an address on 'the recent progress of Women's Trade Societies', where she referred to there being three different kinds of society: 'One kind paid in for strike pay only; a second for strike pay and out of work pay; and a third for strike pay, out of work pay, and provident pay.' Miss Holyoake felt it was a mistake to only offer pay if workers were on strike, as it caused 'a good deal of agitation', with members then wanting to go on strike all the time![6]

In the 1820s, the temperance movement – advocating abstinence from hard spirits, primarily – began to take a hold in both Britain and America, with the 1830s seeing a substantial growth in temperance societies and groups, with the simultaneous emergence of teetotalism as a harder line temperance movement. By the late 1840s, campaigning efforts were increasingly focused on 'saving' the working class and their children, on reducing the reliance on pubs and the influence of pub culture. The temperance movement became a mass movement, although still linked with religion – early proponents of temperance, such as Reverend Jabez Tunnicliff in Leeds and Reverend John Edgar in Belfast, had made this clear. Therefore, meetings were often held in churches, and combined the argument for temperance or teetotalism with Christian teachings. Other organisations were started over the course of the later nineteenth century, which had various degrees of attitude towards drinking (from reducing heavy drinking to banning alcohol), but all of which were critical of some aspect of it.

On 2 June 1887, the British Women's Temperance Association held a meeting at St Aldates Rectory Room, with the Reverend Cason Christopher in the chair. Here, one woman gave a talk about the effects of alcohol, illustrated with 'facts which had come within her own personal knowledge'. Florence Balgarnie then stressed the magnitude of the problem, and said that it was a 'national evil of wider and deeper importance than any other ... in any given factory, owing to our modern system of division of labour, one dissolute or idle man or woman was capable of delaying or injuring the work of 19 industrious and sober men and women.'[7] It was clear here that alcohol was seen only as a problem when it affected the lower orders of society, because of the impact on their work. But it was also clear that here was an arena where women had a say – unlike with elections. At this meeting, it was noted that many women were opposed to pubs opening on Sundays, and that although 'women householders had no direct and responsible influence as voters … that would come ere long, and even now, they could by letters and interviews impress their views at least upon their own Member [of Parliament].' Already, nearly 4,000 women had signed a petition to the queen asking for the sale of alcohol on Sundays to be stopped.[8]

The Church of England Temperance Society's Women's Union had an Oxford Branch; in 1895, its president was Charlotte Adair (1849–1929), an army major's wife.[9] The Oxford branch held an annual meeting every year – on the afternoon of Tuesday, 7 March 1910, it was held in the hall of Hertford College. 'There was a very good attendance, over which the Archdeacon of Oxford was present'. Women on the platform for the meeting included Miss Florence Anson and Miss Constance Gant, who had, until recently, been honorary secretary of the Women's Union for the Chichester Diocese. The good attendance wasn't enough for the archdeacon, who said he felt the branch should,

> enrol more members and elicit more support, because he thought it was really imperative that everyone who took an interest – and what Christian was there who did not take an interest, more or less? – in temperance work should try to inform themselves of the sphere, and magnitude, and ramifications of the work which the Church of England Society did, in order that they might pass on the information to the great mass of hurch people, who, he was afraid, did not know much of the work that the society did.[10]

However, he was pleased with the recent employment of mission workers. As was often the case, this meeting involved women being talked at by men. The Bishop of Croydon told them that ninety per cent of crime in the country was caused by drink, and that 'the matters brought before the Divorce Court were almost entirely owing to drink, and that poverty mainly originated from the same cause'. But he went even further:

> There was one other matter, which was the most important and serious of all. They [the Royal Commission on the Poor Law] had found that drinking among women was undoubtedly on the increase ... since the year 1875 the increase of deaths among women that were directly attributed to intemperance had increased by the appalling total of 130 per cent.

The Bishop argued that as a result, children were increasingly becoming the victims of 'gross cruelty' – in other words, women who drank were worse than men because it led to them neglecting their domestic and childrearing responsibilities. Women should instead join the temperance society, preferably signing up to total abstinence, thereby 'working by example'. They should also collect money 'as the society very much wanted it'.

Mrs Whittuck, a vicar's wife (presumably Mary Charlotte Whittuck, whose husband Charles was vicar of the University Church of St Mary's), then read the Oxford Branch of the Women's Union's annual report, noting that one woman, Florence Sweet (who in 1911 gave her occupation as 'Women's Union Mission Worker'), had visited over 200 women during the year – those who had stayed off the drink, and those who had faced 'times of special temptation, such as Bank Holidays'. Wives needed to save their husbands; and the avoidance of drink meant better relations with neighbours, and better lives for children. The Branch held a weekly – or almost weekly – temperance meeting for working women, hosted by Miss Sweet, in St Paul's parish. The meeting tended to take place on a Friday evening – when many had finished work and might otherwise be tempted to take a drink or two to celebrate the weekend. Instead, they were offered tea and cake by volunteers.

It was, though, recognised that many women were not interested in the temperance movement. Constance Gant, who had previously been honorary secretary of the Chichester Diocese Women's Union, commented that although the Women's Union was seen as a power for education, they needed to get more 'cultured, thinking women to take an interest'. She added,

> There is so much ignorance and prejudice that clings around the word 'temperance' that it is very hard indeed to get ladies to go to temperance meetings. We always find that when people become introduced, the first question they ask is, 'What can we do?' Each locality has to find suitable work for its members. We ask for a little more enthusiasm in fighting against the evil of intemperance.[11]

Even these female members saw other women who drank as worse than their male counterparts, with Miss Gant stating that,

> if the mothers of England drank, it meant that they passed on the terrible heritage to their children, who were born with predisposition to this dreadful vice; they were deficient in will power and in physical and mental stamina.... If the women of England deteriorated it meant the deterioration of the race. If the home life of the nation was set in a lower key it must affect the religious and moral life of the nation ... women should understand not only the evil but their responsibility in the matter.[12]

By this time, though, the temperance movement was past its peak, and was achieving some of its goals, thus taking the fire out of its campaigning. Two years earlier, the Prime Minister, Herbert Asquith, had proposed to close thousands of pubs across England and Wales, only to be defeated by the Conservatives, who had seen brewers protest the proposals. However, in 1910, pubs were faced with a hefty tax under what was known as the People's Tax, and in the two decades between 1900 and 1920, the consumption of beer and other alcoholic drinks halved as pubs faced competition with other means of relaxation outside of work. After the outbreak of the first world war, the Defence of the Realm Act was passed and this resulted in the licensing of pub opening hours, the weakening in strength of beer, and an extra penny tax on every pint. By the 1930s, the movement was declining.

Another form of society in Oxford was the friendly society. Friendly societies had been in existence since at least the late eighteenth century, providing support not just for working men but also for their families. Many of these societies were run by the gentry, but they were aimed at helping those less fortunate.[13] These societies might give money directly to those in need, but they might also offer goods, such as coal or shoes. Women subscribed to these societies, and supported local charities, but the societies were not designed specifically for them. In the 1880s however, the Oxford Charity Organisation Society 'was central to the creation and subsequent development' of one local society designed for women – the Oxford Working Women's Benefit Society, which in 1892, was commended for having 'worked steadily in Oxford for the last 10 years'.[14] The Oxford COS believed that everyone should be able to join friendly societies or sick clubs, regardless of how poor they were, as a way of avoiding the seeking of poor relief.[15] The idea was popular, and it gave women a purpose in terms of organising such societies on a day-to-day basis, even if they did not need its help at that point: Daniel Weinbren has estimated that by the 1890s, there were 20,000 women working in a paid capacity for philanthropic societies.[16]

In Oxford, there was a diocesan branch of the Women's Help Society, which was unsurprisingly headed by the Bishop of Oxford, one of the society's two presidents, along with a Mrs Stubbs. This society had a subset of 'lady workers', and a Travelling Secretary, Miss Mackenzie. She gave the society's work and object as being to 'band together by parochial associations and simple rule of life, women and girls of all classes, to help them to lead a higher religious life.'[17] Another local society was the Protective and Provident Society of Women working in trades in the city, which was established in around 1882 by Emily Pattison (the wife of Mark Pattison) and others.[18] It held an annual meeting each year that was attended by the key movers and shakers in improving the lives of working women.[19] In 1886, the meeting was held in the girls' schoolroom on Blackfriars Road on the evening of Thursday, 11 November, following a well-attended tea. The meeting was attended by the deputy mayor of Oxford, Alderman Buckell, and Henry Nettleship – the local newspaper, the *Oxford Journal*, only saw fit to mention the key men involved. The chairman for the evening was the president of Trinity College, who commended the members for the fact that the society 'had taken such a firm root in Oxford', despite the city's small population – then around 40,000. However, he noted that 'it would be a good thing for the working women of Oxford if the numbers were increased'. The aim of the society was to increase the comfort, security and happiness of local working women – to give them 'a sense of security which would last for a good many years'. If they encountered financial problems, the society's funds would be able to help them out. In addition, the society's teas, entertainments and other meetings were designed to offer working women 'something to brighten their lives – pleasant evenings and happy feelings to take back to their homes'.

Although some of the statements of men and women involved in such societies could sound patronising, they came from a good place, and in this case, Trinity's president noted that the upper classes recognised that the working classes didn't have as 'bright' a life as they should in a first-world country, and that the richer members of society should help them, rather than ignore them.[20] This was all well and good; however, he was applauded when he then suggested that working women also needed to be more virtuous, exhibiting 'cleanliness, neatness, personal tidiness, cheerfulness, good temper', in order to make their own homes a better place. Members of the society were encouraged to 'spread virtue among their neighbours', for 'if one were to see them in their homes, they kept their homes neat, clean and tidy, and when their husbands were coming home kept up their appearance, and made the homes more cheerful for their reception.'[21] There was therefore confusion as to whether the society was simply trying to give working women a leg up, or whether they wanted to improve their morals and make them better to please their husbands. At this 1886 meeting, the deputy mayor, ignoring the fact that the chair was a man and had suggested that women should improve themselves for the benefit of their husbands, stated that he was deeply curious about the existence of 'a society of women, officered by women, for the distinct advantage of women, and in every respect one that was originated, and was carried on, and was being conducted by, women.'[22]

The 1891 annual meeting of the society offers a useful analysis of its members, and what they paid to be part of the society. The meeting itself was held on a Tuesday evening in November, at the Wesleyan Lecture Room, and despite the dark autumn evening, between seventy and eighty members attended for a sit-down tea. Women present included a 'Miss Foley MA of London, who attended as a Women's Trades Union's [sic] Committee', Mrs Nettleship (who had been in the society since at least 1886), and honorary secretary Miss Farrant, who reported that at the start of 1891, there had been seventy-nine paying members of the society. During the year, fourteen had joined, twelve had left, and two (Mrs Randall and Miss Tyrrell) had died.[23] The society had given twenty-four members a sick allowance (totalling £28 4s 6d) and a further two allowances as they were out of work, which totalled £1 8s. The society kept its money in the Post Office Savings Bank, and currently had nearly £140 there. Miss Foley then spoke of the 'advantages of combination among women'; a Mr King of the Typographical Association (possibly Jonathan King, the London-based stationer), was present and proposed 'that this meeting rejoices in the spread of trades unionism among women during the last two years', commenting that 'men recognised that women had a right to work in any trade, but they thought that women should receive the same proportion of wages as men, because otherwise they would have a deteriorating effect on the rate of wages.'[24]

In February 1895, the society's annual meeting was held at the Wesleyan Lecture Room, with an alderman – barrister and Oxford University law tutor John Charles Wilson – presiding, joined by many of Oxford's wives – including Wilson's own wife, Elizabeth.[25] One woman gave an address about the working conditions of women in the North of England; and the Reverend William Duggan, vicar of St Paul's in Jericho, called on the women present to become 'true missionaries' and encourage other women to sign up by stressing the benefits of membership.[26] His talk also emphasised the importance of self-help: the society 'would only flourish in the truest sense when it had come to live, not only self-governed, but self-extending, valuing all sympathy, but really independent of fostering and encouragement outside, a true organ of a wholesome, thoughtful, earnest, self-respecting life.'[27]

Another similar Oxford society, as previously referred to, was the Oxford Working Women's Benefit Society, who also held an annual meeting at the Wesleyan Lecture Room in 1891. Their meeting, presided over by Henry Nettleship, was held on a Thursday evening in February, where it was noted that 'it was very gratifying to reflect how long they had been in existence – flourishing existence', with the fact that they must have continued to be in existence because of women's continuing want and economic struggle apparently passing them by. Conversely, though, the society's finances were reported to be 'in a very prosperous and satisfactory condition'. Many women had been affected in some way by that year's influenza epidemic; it was also a period when many had been asking 'social questions', with various social schemes being mooted, and Charles Booth's work causing waves not just in London but across the nation. One speaker at the Working Women's Benefit Society meeting stated:

> If General Booth, or any other social reformer, could manage to make those people work who now refused to work, could make those who were profligate to be steady, those who were indolent industrious, those who were restless quiet, those who were irreligious religious, and those who were immoral moral, everybody would wish God-speed to his scheme.[28]

This society reported that at the start of the previous year, it had 125 paying members, with 21 new members joining, and 14 either leaving to ceasing to be members after failing to pay their subs. Twenty-seven women had received a sick allowance from the society, which amounted to £26 12s 6d. It now had 133 paying members, and £264 in reserves. Each parish had its own assistant secretary for the society – the assistant secretary for St Clement's and Cowley, for example, was Sarah Woodward, a grocer's wife who lived at 236 Cowley Road.[29] One member, a Mrs Johnston, proposed that the meeting, cordially approves the efforts now being made by women to secure for themselves in sickness by means of prudently managed Societies such as the Oxford Working Women's Benefit Society. She was very glad that they were waking up to the fact that women were sometimes ill as well as men; also that when they were sick they wanted better food; and further that they liked to provide it for themselves, and not to depend upon some chance friend.

The society was regarded as a 'help yourself' association; there were always those who helped themselves to the money of their friends, but this was a different type of help, whereby people put money into the society to keep it going, and when they needed help when they were sick, they were simply taking out their own money, not someone else's. In this way, it was both a form of savings, and a communal pot of money that helped out anyone who was in genuine need.[30]

Philanthropic women recognised the dangers that faced others of their gender, and attempted to help them. In 1883, the Oxford Ladies' Association for the Care of Friendless Girls, or LACFG, was founded, one of a number of regional branches.[31] It aimed to help and protect both girls and women under the age of 26 – 'the prevention rather than the cure only, of the evils to which they were exposed'. The organisation was partly funded by the Oxford Board of Guardians – in 1900, at a meeting of the Board at the workhouse, 'the usual subscription of £10' was agreed, after being proposed by Charlotte Toynbee.[32]

The LACFG provided a Clothing Club, a free registry for women seeking jobs as domestic servants (in 1900, 127 applications had been made to it, and the society didn't have enough girls to fill all the positions), and also a training home that would provide them with temporary accommodation or training for a domestic service role.[33] This home changed location over the four decades that the LACFG existed; for example, in the 1890s, it was variously based on Walton Street, and Southmoor Road, before moving to Leckford Road and, until the outbreak of the first world war, 108 Woodstock Road. While at 29 Leckford Road, some fifteen girls could be accommodated, not just from Oxford but also from nearby villages. They were asked to pay between 2s 6d and 5s a week, but if they were completely destitute, the LACFG's funds would cover their maintenance. Often, local people would donate money to cover a girl's maintenance, too. It was said that the 'doors of the house in Leckford Road are never shut.'[34] However, the First World War had a negative impact on the organisation, as the privations caused by war meant that people were giving less money to charity, and the society struggled to fundraise enough money. The training home therefore finally closed its doors in September 1914.

One branch of the LACFG visited 'fallen' girls – those who had got pregnant outside of marriage – and arranged, in some cases, for their babies to be looked after elsewhere. In 1898, a home for unmarried mothers and their babies was opened, and christened Hope Cottage; it closed in 1900, and was something of an experiment, designed to see if there was a need for such a home. However, in October 1901, St Frideswide's Cottage, at 59 St John's Road, was rented by the LACFG and opened as a home similar to Hope Cottage. It was run by a 'lady matron' with help from an under-matron, and at any one time, six girls and their babies could be accommodated.[35] Between 1907 and 1919, the organisation's treasurer was Judith Merivale, with a Mrs M. A. Whitaker succeeding her; the association itself closed in 1920.[36]

The organisation, during its relatively short history, put on various forms of fundraising entertainment; in November 1902, for example, it held a performance 'in Mr Taphouse's music room'. Coverage of this concert made explicit the schism between the genteel, intellectual picture of Oxford that tourists still believe today, and the poverty and struggles that lay underneath that façade:

> The Oxford Ladies' Association for the Care of Friendless Girls is one of those unostentatious good works going on in Oxford – works the number of which would surprise the casual visitor, who only sees our beautiful city from the outside, and naturally has no time to consider that behind the beauty Oxford is no more exempt than any other city of the same size from social difficulties and dangers... In Oxford itself

are a GFS Lodge, an Industrial Home and Orphanage, an Orphan and Industrial School, a House of Refuge, a Penitentiary, each connected with various societies and parishes, and the Training Home and Rescue Home – separate houses – in connection with the...LACFG.[37]

Although many women are named in reports of these associations and societies, various names are repeated, showing that although some women had an involvement with a particular organisation, or were only involved on the fringes, others joined several organisations, or were more active participants. Matilda Nettleship's name is one of those mentioned more than once; Mrs Liddell and Lady Samuelson, wife of Sir Bernhard Samuelson MP also.[38]

These were primarily educated women from middle- or upper-middle class families. Often, they were married to academics at the university, and/or the daughters of academics or public school teachers and masters. They had grown up in households where newspapers and books would have been read, where politics may have been debated at the dinner table; and where they wanted something to challenge them and use their own able brains. The options open to them were still fairly limited, but by joining organisations that aimed to help less fortunate women, they found a way of satisfying that need to help, and to find intellectual, yet practical, occupations.

Oxford women were involved with many different societies, as has already been seen. Some were established in Oxford alone, whereas others were local branches of national organisations. In 1903, for example, Jennie Adams was honorary superintendent of the Girls' Friendly Society (Oxford Lodge), based at 36 George Street; in 1914, there was an Oxford branch of the Women's Home Missions Association.[39] Another example of a woman who wanted to improve local society was Agnes Grace Weld. She was born in London in 1849, the niece of Alfred, Lord Tennyson, and as a child was a photographic muse to both Lewis Carroll and Julia Margaret Cameron. She moved to Oxford with her parents, where, in 1891, the family lived just two doors away from another active local citizen, Georgina Müller, in Norham Gardens. At another point living elsewhere in Oxford, on the Iffley Road, in 1901 she gave her occupation as 'living on own means; work among the poor'.

There were also one-off schemes and collections organised by local women, such as in 1887, when Queen Victoria was about to celebrate her Golden Jubilee. The mayoress, Jane Hughes, organised a 'meeting of ladies' at the town hall on a Thursday afternoon, to discuss how to make a jubilee offering to the queen on the part of Oxford women.[40] The meeting was not well attended, although reports were keen to state that this was because of a 'rather inconvenient hour' (2 p.m.) chosen for the meeting, rather than anti-monarchist feeling. Several women did manage to attend to join the mayoress on the platform, including 'Mrs A. W. Hall' – the former Emma Jowett, whose husband was MP for Oxford – Mrs Liddell, and Georgina Müller.[41] The aim, the mayoress stated, was to set up a committee in Oxford that would help collect 'an offering' (money) from individuals, which would form a gift from the women and girls of England to the queen. Speaking to the small audience, she 'trusted that she might have their support and that of all the women and girls of Oxford'.

However, rather than rely on the wealthier, educated women who formed her audience, she wanted the working-classes to support the cause: 'Her chief subscribers would probably be the provident or hard-working women who belonged to the Women's Trade Society and a Sick Benefit Society here in Oxford, some of the very few of the true self-help kind which existed in England for women.' Whether she was counting on strong pro-monarchist feeling among the working-classes, or rather naïvely failed to realise that working women might not be able to afford to spend money on a gift for arguably the nation's wealthiest widow, is not known.[42]

Meanwhile, in the early years of the twentieth century, Oxford's women also established an association arguing for tariff reforms. In 1910, as was usual with such societies, it held a meeting that started with a large tea, attended by 300 women. The meeting was held at the Masonic Buildings on the High Street, and so the food was served by the building's proprietor, George Gardiner. After tea was finished, the tables were removed, and the seats rearranged ready for a 'musical entertainment'. More women now turned up, so that the entertainment was attended by such a large audience that the gallery was 'nearly filled'. Coverage of the event focused, perhaps inevitably, on the entertainment rather than the meeting – which took place between the tea and the entertainment – at which speeches were made, and notable local women including Lady Gray, Miss Courtenay Bell, Mrs Montagu Burrows, Mrs Kennett-Hayes and Miss Sinclaire Rohde [*sic*] were invited onto the platform.[43] The latter name is particularly interesting; the India-born Eleanour Sinclair Rohde (1881–1950) is better remembered today as a garden historian and horticulture writer, but at this time, she was actively involved in women's politics, and in the 1911 census described herself as a lecturer for the Women's Unionist Organisation. After the First World War, the organisation would become the Women's National Advisory Committee.[44]

The 1870 Education Act enabled women to vote for the school boards that provided elementary education in local areas, as well as letting them stand to be members of those school boards. In 1870, four women were elected to local school boards – Flora Stevenson, Lydia Becker, Emily Davies and Elizabeth Garrett, the latter in Marylebone, London.[45] In 1872, Eleanor Smith (1823–1896) was listed as being at a meeting of the Oxford School Board, where she seconded a motion for cheques to be drawn to pay various bills.[46] She was still on the school board in December four years later, attending the monthly meeting at 2 St Aldate's. She was the first member of the board, and still the only one four years after first being elected.[47]

It was not until 1933, however, that a woman took on Oxford's main civic position – that of city mayor. It was Lily Sophia Tawney (1867–1947) who became Oxford's first female mayor, having already been a city councillor for fifteen years, and an Alderman for four. A descendant of the Tawney brewing family, and daughter of a Merton College graduate, Lily had long been involved in the city's political and civic life, and was also involved in its residents' welfare, being on the Board of Guardians and chair of the Public Assistance Committee.[48] Awarded an OBE in the New Year's

Honours list of 1939, she resigned as mayor in 1942, five years before her death.⁴⁹

Women's lives in nineteenth- and twentieth-century Oxford cannot, of course, be considered without looking at the suffrage movement and its operation at both local and national level. The campaign for women's suffrage had gained traction in the second half of the nineteenth century, with women becoming increasingly politically active during campaigns to reform suffrage more generally. John Stuart Mill, a supporter of female suffrage, became an MP in 1865 and argued for an amendment to the 1832 Reform Act to include females voting; a test case in Manchester around the same time – following on from Manchester shopkeeper Lily Maxwell being put on the electoral roll by mistake in the belief that she was a man – argued that the references to males in legislation was vague enough for women to be allowed to vote, too – an argument that was rejected. In 1869, the Municipal Franchise Act was passed, enabling single women who were also ratepayers to vote. In 1894, the Local Government Act extended this right to include some married women. Meanwhile, campaign groups for women's suffrage were being established with the aim of gaining support for the cause from Westminster MPs. In 1897, seventeen groups formed the National Union of Women's Suffrage Societies, and in 1907, the NUWSS organised a large procession through London of 3,000 women to highlight their cause. In 1903, part of the NUWSS membership broke away from the union to form the Women's Social and Political Union (WSPU), under the leadership of Emmeline Pankhurst. It followed an increasingly violent programme.

Back in 1859, the Oxford Debating Society had debated universal suffrage, in an event that excited so much interest that it was attended by the Prince of Wales. However, it accepted an amendment proposed by Sir Rowland Blennerhassett of Christ Church that 'universal suffrage is not desirable, and that no Reform Bill will be complete without a property qualification'.⁵⁰ Judging by the press coverage of the 1860s, suffrage was more of an issue in terms of male suffrage at this point, with 'manhood suffrage' frequently being referred to.⁵¹ However, by the early 1870s, female suffrage was increasingly being discussed in the Oxfordshire papers. On 29 April 1872, a meeting was held in London's Regent Street to promote the National Society for Women's Suffrage, with St George's Hall being 'densely packed' by half an hour before the advertised start. The meeting was covered in Oxfordshire, with the *Banbury Advertiser*, for example, noting the opinions of speakers that denying women the vote was an injustice not only to women, but to men, as it 'trained them' to be selfish, while encouraging women to be 'childish' and only think of trivial things rather than important subjects such as politics.[52]

In April 1878, a women's suffrage meeting was held at the Oxford corn exchange – in the yard of the old town hall – 'to consider the question of extending the parliamentary suffrage to women householders' – again with several male speakers, but also with Lilias Ashworth Hallett and her husband Thomas Hallett, Lydia Becker and Helena Paulina Downing (the latter had spoken at a meeting of the Women's Protective and Provident League in London, in 1875, which aimed to discuss forming a cooperative association for dressmakers, mantle-makers and other needlewomen, where she argued that it was not charity women needed, but self-reliance and independence).[53] Lilias Ashworth Hallett stated that the number of female householders in Oxford was around 750 – one-seventh of the entire constituency. These women were taxpayers, and therefore should be allowed to vote.[54] As mention of the likes of Hallett, Becker and Downing suggests, many of those involved in the suffrage movement were also involved with other organisations, all aiming to improve women's lives, whether in terms of work or politics, and also lectured and campaigned on the issue of women's suffrage around the country. Helena, later Helena Downing Shearer, was a long-term member of the Suffrage Society, and later lectured on behalf of the society as well as organising its meetings, before dying prematurely in London in 1885, aged 45.[55] Lydia Becker (1827–1890), also mentioned here, was from Manchester, and had convened the Manchester Women's Suffrage Committee back in 1867, speaking at the first public meeting of the National Society for Women's Suffrage in the city the following year.

Lilias Ashworth Hallett (1844–1922) had joined the London Society for Women's Suffrage in 1867, and later became a supporter of the WSPU – until it started to resort to arson in 1912 – and was a close friend of Lydia Becker.[56] In 1880, both Helena and Lydia supported a resolution put forward at the St Andrew's Hall in Norwich to put a petition to the House of Commons stating that 'properly qualified Women should be relieved from the Electoral Disabilities under which they now labour'.[57] Local groups were incentivised by these campaigners, who attended meetings, speaking eloquently about women's suffrage, and galvanising local men and women into action.

In 1887, the Oxford press was still covering the issue of suffrage locally; Yorkshire suffragist Florence Balgarnie (1856–1928) had given a lecture arguing for women's suffrage to the Oxford Reform Club in this year, and the *Oxford Times* referred to this, arguing that women might be good for politics, as 'their bias undoubtedly lies towards religion, morality and sobriety'. Yet already, prior to the violence advocated by the WSPU in the early twentieth century, it was condemning more radical women for their 'tall talk and egotism', which could have the effect of damaging people's perceptions of suffrage.[58] The *Oxford Times* also only believed in suffrage for single women – 'We are not advocating the enfranchisement of married women, we leave them to be represented by their husbands.'[59] Two years later, the University Union's Debating Rooms again held a debate on women's suffrage, showing that this was an increasingly important issue that was not going to go anywhere soon.[60]

The Oxford Women's Liberal Association was established in February 1888 and held its first general meeting on 10 October that year at the Liberal Hall. This was presided over by Professor James Legge – the university's first professor of Chinese – with an address given by Florence Balgarnie. Also present were the honorary secretary, Miss Macdonald, as well as a significant number of women, including:

> Mrs Sidgwick, Mrs Massie, Mrs Macdonald, Mrs Rhys, Mrs Amphlett, Mrs and Miss Harley, Mrs James, Mrs Unwin, Mrs Kingerlee,

Mrs Beesley, Mrs Mansell, Mrs G Evans, Miss Taylor, Mrs Adams, Miss Mathews, Mrs Spencer, Miss Goodwin, Miss Cooper, Miss Payne, Mrs Egan, etc.[61]

Tragically, between the time of the society being established, and its general meeting eight months later, the society's first secretary, Flora Lindsay Ritchie (née Macdonell), the 29-year-old wife of David Ritchie, a fellow and tutor of Jesus College, had died; the couple had lived at 39 Banbury Road. After her death there, which followed a 'painful illness', on 24 July 1888, Flora made the headlines of several newspapers. She had desired to be cremated – an unusual request for the time – and so, after a service at the Ritchie home that was attended by the Master of Balliol and Max Müller among many others, she was cremated at the Cremation Society of England's premises in Surrey. Flora's coffin was transported down to Surrey covered in floral wreaths, including one sent by the Oxford Women's Liberal Association.[62]

Because of Flora's untimely death, Miss Macdonald had become the Oxford Women's Liberal Association's secretary.[63] It was this lady who gave a speech at the association's general meeting, saying:

> For some time, there had been a growing desire among the women of Oxford for the formation of an association of this kind, and at a time when many such associations were being formed in different parts of England it was felt very desirable that they should take their part in the general movement. Both City and University had cordially co-operated in the work. ... The number of members, which has shown a very satisfactory increase, is now 230, the original number having been 71, and of these, nearly one half are working women, who thus prove their interest in the matters connected with the national welfare.[64]

Professor Legge said he 'rejoiced' that women were taking such an interest in England's institutions, and with improving their social and political life. But yet again, he related this to their relationships with men: 'Man was not complete in himself socially – it was not good for him to be alone. Man was not complete in himself politically either', and so if he combined his 'physical vigour and masculine energy' with women's 'quicker feeling, greater power of sympathy [and] more kindly emotional nature', it would be good both for the administration of public affairs, and the country.[65]

In 1899, a meeting was held by the similarly-named Women's Liberal Government Society – a non-party organisation set up to promote the eligibility of women to elect and serve on all local government bodies – to consider the position of women in the London Government Bill that was currently before government. Mary Stewart Kilgour had come to Oxford to London to speak, and education campaigner Mary-Jane Bridges Adams had also attended. More locally, the meeting was attended by three Oxford councillors as well as socially aware Oxford women such as the Misses Adair (sisters Beatrice and Helen; Helen had taken her Oxford University examinations nine years earlier), Charlotte Toynbee, and the suffragist Mrs Eagleston, who would later set up an NUWSS circle in St Ebbes.[66]

The Oxford Women's Suffrage Society, which was founded in 1904, was part of the National Union of Women's Suffrage Societies, and key members included Jessie Payne Margoliouth (née Smith, 1856–1933), who had married David Margoliouth, laudian professor of Arabic, at the age of 40 in 1896, and Maude Royden (a former student at Lady Margaret Hall).[67] In October 1909, it held a 'well-attended' meeting at the Assembly Room of the Town Hall on St Aldate's. It was keen to involve working-class women, and put a call out to local shop assistants to get involved. Ironically, given its mission – to give women a voice – the meeting was presided over by a man, the Oxford law professor William Geldart. However, three women – Lady Mary Murray (who was president of the Oxford Women's Liberal Association from 1891–1901), Winifred Haverfield, and Vera Farnell – spoke.[68]

They discussed the fact that women were perceived to be far more ignorant than they really were; that many of them worked because they needed a wage, rather than simply wanting 'pocket money', and that the status of women's work therefore needed to be raised. A resolution was passed that women should be 'immediately' enfranchised on equal terms to men, and a record of this was sent to the prime minister.[69] The following June, the society sent a petition to the prime minister, 'begging' for the government 'to afford facilities for the discussion and divisions necessary to the passage of Mr Shackleton's Representation of the People Bill through the House of Commons'.[70] It was signed by many men, including the Provost of Queen's College, the Warden of Wadham College, various professors, the mayor, aldermen, and other well-qualified locals, their MAs and other qualifications proudly listed.[71]

Myfanwy Rhys, who had attended the Oxford High School for Girls from 1884 to 1890, grew up to become the first secretary of the Oxford Women's Suffrage Society, holding the role until 1907, while another student, Margaret Sidgwick, was later on the executive committee of the National Union of Women's Suffrage Societies.[72] The link between town and gown, and the influence of education and mixing in intellectual circles, in terms of political and social activism, was a strong one.

However, the strong calls for suffrage from Oxford residents were not universal. There was opposition to female suffrage too, with the Anti-Women's Suffrage Movement holding a protest against the Votes for Women Bill in the summer of 1910, which was attended by Georgina Müller. This meeting's speakers were keen to point out that they did not think women to be inferior to men – in fact, they regarded them as superior in some ways – but that women *were* 'inferior from a business and political point of view', and that men were not 'prepared to subject themselves to petticoat government'. The rather illogical point of view presented in this protest was that the 'ultimate consequence' of giving women the vote was that women would control men – and that women's rule would mean 'the end of the Empire'.[73] Although to us such arguments seem absurd, they do remind us that a century ago, not only were many men against female suffrage, but so too were some women, and the status quo was desired by those protesting against the fight for women's suffrage.

Another expression of this fear of women being given the vote came in 1912 – by which point the Oxford Women's Suffrage Society had over 400 members. A suffrage rally was held in St Giles, led by Sylvia Pankhurst, but the event did not go smoothly.[74] Sylvia was said to have been pelted with stones by students from St John's College, causing her to make her escape in a cab. In the January of 1913, a torchlit procession had been held from Cowley Place to St Giles, with various suffrage societies and supporters taking part. On 19 July, suffragists who were marching from Carlisle to London reached Oxford; they arrived in Summertown in the late afternoon, with banners flying, and were met by Oxford suffragists, who took them for tea before the procession continued on to St Giles. A spell at the Lamb and Flag pub followed, before a suffrage meeting was held at the town hall.[75] Also that year, boathouses were set on fire, and students from Magdalen College destroyed a women's club.

The objectors, however, were increasingly in a minority, and times were changing. The war came and everything changed. In February 1918, the Representation of the People Act was passed, enabling over 8 million women above the age of 30 to gain the vote, provided they met certain property qualifications. In November that year, women could become MPs for the first time, after the Parliament (Qualification of Women) Act was passed; but it wasn't until 1928 that a further Representation of the People Act gave the vote to all women aged over 21. It was at this point that the start of a more progressive, modern life beckoned for Oxford's women.

Conclusion

This book has only been able to touch on aspects of women's lives in Oxford over the past couple of centuries, yet it has shown, I hope, that these lives were more diverse than might be expected from a city so associated with its university and constituent colleges. At the heart of Oxford's social and political life over the nineteenth and first half of the twentieth centuries were, perhaps predictably, those from the affluent middle-classes – the women who were the daughters or wives of vicars or academics, living in or around the area of Norham Gardens, and wanting to be involved in as many aspects of life as they were able to. Prior to being able to take Oxford degrees, they still fought for the right for an education at the same level as men's; to educate their daughters; to develop their political nous and awareness through various campaigning activities, including suffrage. Women also helped other women, taking on roles that enabled them to help those less fortunate – those who had illegitimate children, who had 'fallen', or who simply had few financial resources.

And what of those women further down the social ladder? These women played an active role in Oxford life as well. They were the women who worked in the city's many businesses, in its shops, cafes, hotels, publishers, and for the university, as the proprietors of lodging houses or as cleaners. Some women helped their male family members out with their businesses, but others were proud business owners themselves, keeping their families afloat, contributing to the family economy, and managing budgets, staff and property. They made sure the city ran smoothly and that those within it were able to buy, sell, learn and live. They socialised, too, and over time frequented bars, coffee shops and cafes, temperance hotels, the theatre and the cinema. Twice during the period covered in this book, Oxford was disrupted by war, but although there were changes during this time, both in terms of university life changing, men being absent through war, and different rules, including rationing, having an impact on everyone's lives, other aspects remained the same: working, caring, feeding, entertaining and being entertained, making and maintaining friendships and relationships.

Change occurred in different ways, too. Most obviously, women became able first to take Oxford university exams, and then to gain a degree. They gained the vote; they were able to take on civic and political positions. Their worlds opened up, although they had to continue – and still continue today – to fight entrenched male attitudes towards their increased participation in aspects of life seen historically as a male preserve. The treatment of mental health issues has changed for the better over time, and women have also benefited from improved medical care, less risky childbirth and better support in times of need. Women in Oxford today may be able to do more than their predecessors, but they still have plenty in common with them. Some aspects of life are universal, and our desire to make our communities better, to improve the aspects that need it, and to live our lives to the fullest remain. Just as the likes of Mrs Liddell and Mrs Toynbee got involved in city life, both social and political, so too do many women today. Oxford is, and has always been, about more than the dreaming spires and the male dons traditionally associated with it; it has always been about its women, too – the women with their own dreams and active lives within the city. This book has been about them, in recognition of what they achieved, whether on a small or a large scale.

References

Introduction
1. Malcolm Graham, 'The Suburbs of Victorian Oxford: Growth in a Pre-Industrial City' (PhD thesis, University of Leicester, 1985), 1, accessed via http://www.jerichocentre.org.uk/images/about/1985Grahammphd-2.pdf
2. Ibid
3. Ibid., 14
4. Liz Woolley, 'The coming of the railway to Oxford', South Oxford Community Centre website (http://www.southoxford.org/local-history-in-south-oxford/interesting-aspects-of-grandpont-and-south-oxford-s-history/the-coming-of-the-railway-to-oxford)

Chapter 1: Education
1. Angela Goddard, 'Doing English Language: A Guide for Students' (Routledge, 2012), p.4, referencing WB Stephens 'Education in Britain 1750-1914' (Macmillan, 1998).
2. 'Women and teaching', Wales History, BBC (http://www.bbc.co.uk/wales/history/sites/themes/society/women_teaching.shtml)
3. http://oxfordhigh.gdst.net/senior-school/ss-about-us/. The Girls' Day School Trust has been founded in 1872 by Maria Grey and her sister, a Miss Shirreff, and by 1891, the trust operated 36 schools nationwide (Vera Brittain, *The Women at Oxford; A Fragment of History*, 31).
4. *Reading Mercury*, 6 February 1875
5. *Oxford Journal*, 25 September 1875
6. *Oxford Journal*, 9 October 1875
7. *Oxford Journal*, 30 December 1876

8. *Oxford Times*, 11 January 1879
9. Pauline Adams, *Somerville for Women Oxford College 1879–1993*, 7
10. Ibid., 8
11. Janet Howarth, 'Sidgwick, Arthur (1840–920)', Oxford Dictionary of National Biography; Keith Hannabuss, 'Smith, Henry John Stephen (1826-1883)', Oxford Dictionary of National Biography
12. Pauline Adams, *Somerville for Women: An Oxford College 1879–1993*, 9
13. Ibid., 11
14. W. J. Mander, *British Idealism: A History* (OUP, 2011), 520; http://www.ox.ac.uk/about/oxford-people/women-at-oxford
15. http://www.st-annes.ox.ac.uk/about/history
16. Keith Hannabuss, 'Eleanor Elizabeth Smith (1822–1896)', Oxford Dictionary of National Biography
17. Pauline Adams, *Somerville for Women*, 18, 27
18. Deborah Manley, *Women in Oxford*, 23
19. Ibid., 12
20. *Reading Mercury*, 28 October 1871
21. Vera Brittain, *The Women at Oxford: A Fragment of History*, 48
22. tweet from Lady Margaret Hall(www.twitter.com/lmhoxford) on 9 March 2017
23. Pauline Adams, *Somerville for Women*, 30
24. Ibid., 7
25. *Guardian*, 21 February 1883, 13
26. Deborah Manley, *Women in Oxford*, 22
27. Pauline Adams, *Somerville for Women*, 9
28. *Portsmouth Evening News*, 13 October 1890
29. *Reading Mercury*, 26 July 1879
30. He held the position at University College until 1881, and later became Dean of Westminster – see 'Oxford Men and Their Colleges, 1880–1892', p. 28, on Ancestry.
31. www.parksandgardens.org/places-and-people/person/1167
32. *The Scotsman*, 11 March 1896
33. Pauline Adams, *Somerville for Women*, 215
34. Pauline Adams includes a list of rules that existed for women undergraduates in 1921, which include a ban on women going

boating with any male except for her brother, and only being allowed to join a mixed gender society if a member of staff from a women's college could be present at the meetings with her (Pauline Adams, *Somerville for Women*, 234–235).
35. Ibid., 87
36. Ibid., 88
37. Pauline Adams, *Somerville for Women*, 150–152
38. www.bodleian.ox.ac.uk/oua/enquiries/first-woman-graduate. Among the first women to receive Oxford degrees were lawyers Cornelia Sorabji, formerly of Somerville College, Gwyneth Bebb - who had studied law at St Hugh's until 1908 - and Ivy Williams, a student of the Society of Oxford Home Students until 1903 (https://www.st-hughs.ox.ac.uk/celebrating-the-life-of-legal-pioneer-gwyneth-bebb/; http://www.twitter.com/OxfordLawFac, 16 October 2018 and http://www.twitter.com/First100years, 15 October 2018).
39. Pauline Adams, *Somerville for Women*, 163–64. This unfair system, although fiddled with over the years, would remain in place until the 1950s.
40. Ibid., 174, 176
41. Ibid., 176
42. UK Outward Passenger Lists, 1890–1960, departure date 8 September 1925, Liverpool to Boston on the Samaria, on Ancestry
43. Pauline Adams, *Somerville for Women*, 193
44. *Illustrated London News*, 25 March 1961

Chapter 2: Work
1. *Oxford Times*, 24 October 1903
2. Ibid.
3. Pamela Cox and Annabel Hobley, *Shopgirls*, xii
4. Pamela Cox and Annabel Hobley, *Shopgirls*, 23
5. Stephanie Jenkins, 'Oxford History: The High' (http://www.oxfordhistory.org.uk/high/tour/north/010_012.html)
6. The Little Clarendon Street branch had opened by 1903, when it was included in the Kelly's Directory of that year.

7. Pamela Cox and Annabel Hobley, *Shopgirls*, 39
8. Pamela Cox and Annabel Hobley, *Shopgirls*, 99, 110–111
9. Ibid., 110
10. Ibid., 160, 170
11. Pamela Cox and Annabel Hobley, *Shopgirls*, 175
12. *Banbury Advertiser*, 20 May 1942
13. *Oxford Journal*, 20 November 1880
14. See http://global.oup.com/uk/archives/8.html#
15. This does appear to have been Ada's surname, although by the time of her marriage two years later, she signed her name simply as 'Rawlins'.
16. Monsieur D'Egville stated in an advert in 1883 that he had for some years performed with his cousin, 'the late and celebrated Madame Michau, in London' and was still holding dancing, deportment and calisthenics classes for 'the daughters of gentlemen in Oxford'. However, he seems to have actually been living in Edgbaston, Birmingham, at the time (*Oxford Journal*, 15 December 1883).
17. *Oxford Journal*, 9 January 1875
18. Bonnie G Smith, *Changing Lives: Women in European History since 1700*, .203
19. *Oxford Journal*, 30 December 1876
20. *Oxford Journal*, 30 December 1876
21. *Oxford Times*, 10 October 1903
22. *Oxford Journal*, 9 January 1875
23. *Oxford Times*, 10 October 1903
24. *Oxford Journal*, 18 June 1881
25. *Oxford Journal*, 15 December 1883
26. *Oxford Times*, 6 September 1902
27. *Oxford Times*, 20 April 1902
28. *Oxford Times*, 19 November 1910
29. *Oxford Times*, 5 November 1910
30. Ten years earlier, Eliza Hewlett had run her own 'sweet coffee shop' at George Street. Her husband, Philip, appears to have not been involved in her business, instead working as a house decorator.

Chapter 3: Home
1. 11 Geo 3 c.14
2. See Peter Higginbotham, 'Oxford, Oxfordshire' at www.workhouses.org.uk/Oxford/
3. www.workhouses.org.uk/Oxford/#Post-1834
4. It finally closed in 1981, and the buildings eventually demolished (http://www.workhouses.org.uk/Oxford/#Post-1834).
5. 1881 census for Oxford Workhouse, Cowley Road, Oxford
6. Stephanie Jenkins, 'Headington's Newer Estates', http://www.headington.org.uk/history/streets/estates/index.html
7. John Boughton, 'The Blackbird Leys Estate, Oxford: 'Never accepted as part of the city proper" (2013), https://municipaldreams.wordpress.com/2013/05/07/the-blackbird-leys-estate-oxford-never-part-of-the-city-proper/
8. *Oxford Journal*, 1 November 1851
9. *Western Gazette*, 22 October 1937
10. *Oxford Times*, 25 March 1893; Civil Divorce Records, 1858–1916, on Ancestry. One Ancestry user, slapdash051, has noted that Lavinia Jane married the mysterious lover – George B Reynolds – and they emigrated to New Zealand. If this is correct, she died on 10 September 1944 in Christchurch, having outlived both first and second husband (Lavinia J Baker, 1860–1944, shared by user slapdash051 on Ancestry). This user has uploaded a death notice for Lavinia that records her as 'widow of George Bernard Reynolds, Esq, and mother of Major B. T. Reynolds, MC, RA' (source as before).
11. The 1901 census records that Henry was now a boarder at 40 Walton Crescent, working as a compositor, and his landlord may have been his manager or foreman at work, being the printers' overseer John de la Mare.
12. *Swindon Advertiser*, 4 November 1910
13. *Banbury Guardian*, 24 May 1923
14. The 1881 census for 8 Queen Street lists only one child by Walter's first marriage living with him – Herbert W. Biggs, born 1867 in Hampstead; however, in the 1891 census for 8 Queen Street, Walter has three adult children living with him – Walter L Biggs, 33; Helen G. Biggs, 26; and Sidney B. Biggs, 22, all

REFERENCES 115

born in London. Walter is listed as married, but his second wife Lavinia is absent, presumably singing elsewhere. Son Herbert, who would then have been only four years old, is also absent. In the 1881 census for Paddington, a Walter L. Biggs, born London, is working as a bookseller's assistant but his age is given as 28, so this might be a different individual; neither Helen nor Sidney can be found in the 1881 census.
15. *Nottingham Evening Post*, 29 June 1933
16. *Hartlepool Northern Daily Mail*, 5 July 1941
17. The 1911 census for 14 Linton Road, Oxford, records Henry Bickersteth Cooper, 49, living there with his wife Anna Maria, 52, and daughters Audrey Maria and Bertha White, together with a 21-year-old cook, Fanny Church, and housemaid Emily Sophia Faulkner, 19. Henry was a Norfolk man, born in Forncett St Mary in 1861, the fourth son of a rector, but went from Radley College to Keble, where he gained his BA in 1884 and an MA in 1887, before becoming a fellow at Hertford College until 1891 ('Ex-Fellows of Hertford' in 'Oxford Men and their Colleges, 1880-1892, in two volumes', 602, on Ancestry).
18. *Army and Navy Gazette*, 6 April 1912
19. Author's family history
20. Edward Bracher, the father, died in June 1887, aged 64; Susanna, their mother, survived another two decades after her children's deaths, dying at the age of 80 in September 1896

Chapter 4: Food and drink
1. *Banbury Guardian*, 25 May 1905
2. *Oxford Chronicle and Reading Gazette*, 5 March 1853
3. *Oxford Times*, 17 February 1866
4. *Cambridge Independent Press*, 14 April 1866
5. *Oxford Times*, 6 September 1902
6. *Oxford Times*, 5 March 1881
7. *Banbury Guardian*, 13 December 1894
8. www.oxfordhistory.org.uk/old_oxford/east_oxford/st_clements_st.html
9. *Oxford Times*, 4 November 1938
10. *Oxford Times*, 23 January 1904

11. *Oxford Journal*, 8 July 1899
12. *Oxford Times*, 1 June 1895
13. *Oxford Times*, 5 January 1895
14. *Oxford Times*, 11 August 1877; Oxford Times, 7 January 1882
15. *Oxford Times*, 5 January 1895, Oxford Times, 16 March 1895; Oxford Times, 20 April 1895; Oxford Times, 24 March 1883. An advert from 3 February 1883 shows that by this time, the café had expanded to take over numbers 2 and 3 Castle Street as well as number 4, but by 1895, it was only at numbers 3 and 4 (*Oxford Times*, 3 February 1883).
16. *Oxford Times*, 7 November 1896, *Oxford Times*, 24 September 1898 and 3 December 1898
17. *Oxford Times*, 14 May 1898
18. 1939 Kelly's Directory, 258, on Ancestry
19. New Excelsior Café, details as provided on https://address-search.co.uk/business/20017278/New-Excelsior-Cafe-250-Cowley-Road-OXFORD-OX4-1UH/
20. The site was demolished in 1970 (T. G. Hassall, 'Excavations at 44-46 Cornmarket Street, Oxford, 1970', *Oxoniensia* (1971), pp. 15–36). Hassall states that the Cadena was at 44 to 46 Cornmarket Street; the site had originally been four separate properties, that the company then combined to form a single building (p. 19).
21. *Gloucester Citizen*, 29 April 1932; *The Era*, 7 August 1935
22. *Western Daily Press*, 29 August 1930, *Reading Mercury*, 18 March 1939
23. *The Era*, 27 November 1935
24. *Birmingham Daily Gazette*, 8 May 1939
25. *Eastbourne Gazette*, 19 January 1938
26. Sarah and Frank had five children – four boys and a girl, of whom one son died in childhood. Sarah's jam-making was seen perhaps as more of a domestic task than a professional one, but in today's climate, it is certainly jarring that her role in the success of Frank Cooper's is not recognised in the census entries.
27. https://web.archive.org/web/20131205044715/http://www.oxford-coveredmarket.co.uk:80/content/beginnings-1771

28. https://web.archive.org/web/20131205211905/http://www.oxford-coveredmarket.co.uk:80/content/other-business
29. https://web.archive.org/web/20131205211905/http://www.oxford-coveredmarket.co.uk:80/content/other-business
30. *Oxford Chronicle* and *Reading Gazette*, 7 February 1857
31. Information taken from the 1876 Harrod's Directory of Oxfordshire, on Ancestry, 8
32. The 1871 census for 31 Broad Street records Edward H. Payne, 46, as a grocer; there is no occupation listed for his wife, Emily Ann, then aged 43
33. Army News, 14 May 1942, p.1

Chapter 5: Health
1. Snow had first theorised that cholera was not the result of air, but of a mouth-borne factor, back in 1849, when he published 'On the Mode of Communication of Cholera' – however, despite his identification of a contaminated water pump being the source of the 1854 outbreak in Soho, his theory was not widely accepted until the 1860s ('John Snow (1813–1858)', BBC History, www.bbc.co.uk/history/historic_figures/snow_john.shtml). Henry Wentworth Acland was, however, a believer in Snow's contamination theory, and hence the importance he placed on the sewage contamination of Oxford's rivers.
2. 'Oxford history: cholera', at http://oxfordhistory.org.uk/cholera/index.html
3. Henry Wentworth Acland, *Memoir on the cholera at Oxford in the year 1854, with considerations suggested by the epidemic* (John Churchill, London, 1856), 10; 'Cholera', Oxfordshire Health Archives, www.oxfordshirehealtharchives.nhs.uk/tales-from-archive/cholera.htm.
4. Ibid., 13
5. Ibid., 34
6. Ibid., 14. Of course, some from higher up the social ladder did suffer from cholera too; entries in the returns from doctors include an architect, a railway inspector, and an accountant.
7. Ibid., 15
8. Ibid., 29

9. Ibid., 24
10. Malcolm Graham, 'The Suburbs of Victorian Oxford: Growth in a Pre-Industrial City', 13. See also 'Annual reports of the Medical Health of the City of Oxford (1972-1900)', Oxfordshire History Centre.
11. Martha's home was not named by the newspapers beyond it being a 'dark court', but her burial entry for St Thomas the Martyr on 30 December 1867 gives her home address as Wyatt's Yard, St Thomas. The 1851 census records Martha, then aged 49, and her husband James, 56, whose occupation is given as a general labourer, living at Nelson Street in the same parish.
12. *Chelmsford Chronicle*, 10 January 1868
13. *Oxford Times*, 4 January 1868; Reports initially gave her name as Martha Harris, although this was later corrected by a reader of the *Oxford Times* to Sargeant, and the death records record the death of Martha Sargeant.
14. Derek Brown, '1945–51: Labour and the creation of the welfare state', *The Guardian*, 14 March 2001 (www.theguardian.com/politics/2001/mar/14/past.education); 'The history of the NHS in England', https://www.nhs.uk/NHSEngland/thenhs/nhshistory/Pages/NHShistory1948.aspx. Sir William Beveridge proposed that everyone should pay a weekly sum to the state, which would then pay out benefits to those who were sick, jobless, retired, or widowed (The National Archives, 'The Welfare State', www.nationalarchives.gov.uk/pathways/citizenship/brave_new_world/welfare.htm)
15. www.workhouses.org.uk/Oxford/
16. www.workhouses.org.uk/Headington/
17. www.workhouses.org.uk/Oxford
18. Ibid.
19. www.workhouses.org.uk/Oxford/Oxford1881.shtml#Inmates
20. *Oxford Journal*, 3 May 1873. The Great Stink of 1858, in London, had led to long-debated proposals to modernise the capital's sewerage system to be implemented, and the debates about Oxford's drainage may have become more anxious

following this (Javier Abellán, 'Water supply and sanitation services in modern Europe: developments in 19th–20th centuries' (2017, 12th International Conference of Economic History, University of Salamanca), 9.
21. *Oxford Journal*, 5 June 1875
22. *Illustrated Police News*, 29 July 1899; Thomas Malthus, 'An Essay on the Principle of Population' (J. Johnson, London, 1798)
23. 'Our history: to the Manor born', NHS Oxford University Hospitals NHS Foundation Trust, www.ouh.nhs.uk/hospitals/jr/history.aspx
24. Andrew Moss, 'The RI: A Medical History', *Oxford Today* (Trinity issue, 2007), 15; Daily Herald, 12 March 1931
25. *Banbury Advertiser*, 1 July 1937. A memoriam advertisement was placed in the local paper a year after the deaths by Rose's mourning mother, two sisters, Emily and Lizzie, and her brother-in-law, Will. Rose Baker had married Thomas Ramm six years prior to her death. In the 1939 Register, compiled three years after the deaths, Thomas Ramm, a 32-year-old rollerman of aluminium sheets, is described as a widower, living with his parents and two younger brothers in Banbury. There was a happy ending for Thomas, however, as he married again in 1941.
26. *Bucks Herald*, 31 January 1941
27. *Bucks Herald*, 25 December 1931
28. *Lincolnshire Standard and Boston Guardian*, 2 June 1934
29. 'Littlemore Hospital, Oxford', Oxfordshire Health Archives at www.oxfordshirehealtharchives.nhs.uk/hospitals/littlemore_hospital.htm
30. '19th century mental health', Ashford and St Peter's Hospital (2014), www.ashfordstpeters.nhs.uk/19th-century-mental-health
31. See J. Neeleman, 'Suicide as a crime in the UK: legal history, international comparisons and present implications', *Acta Psychiatrica Scandinavica*, 94:4 (1996), 252–257
32. Press reports stated that John Rostron was from Manchester; there is a record of a death of a John Henry Rostron, aged 20, in late 1894, which might well be Kate's fiancé.

33. *Oxford Journal*, 18 August 1894
34. *Warwick and Warwickshire Advertiser*, 19 June 1937. Adelaide Street was where the unmarried Ethel had grown up; the 1901 and 1911 census records her with her family at number 8. She was one of 12 children born to William, a cab driver, and his wife Sarah.

Chapter 6: Leisure
1. *Western Times*, 5 October 1912
2. *Oxford Times*, 29 September 1877
3. *Oxford Times*, 18 October 1862
4. *Oxford Times*, 15 October 1910
5. *Oxford Times*, 2 January 1909
6. *Oxford Times*, 19 December 1908
7. *Oxford Times*, 12 December 1908
8. *Oxford Times*, 14 December 1901
9. In 1958, the two properties – Boswell's on Broad Street and the Oxford Drug Company on Cornmarket Street – were connected internally, and the shop has continued in this format ever since (www.boswells.co.uk/about-us).
10. *Banbury Guardian*, 23 August 1923. The shopping carnival took place between 14 and 22 September.
11. *Illustrated Sporting and Dramatic News*, 27 February 1886
12. www.oxfordhistory.org.uk/george_street
13. *Leicester Chronicle*, 12 March 1898
14. www.arthurlloyd.co.uk/OxfordTheatres/TheatreRoyalOxford.htm
15. *Cambridge Chronicle and Journal*, 4 February 1865
16. Obituary of Edward Hooper, *Oxford Times*, 14 January 1865 – he died on 8 January 1865, aged 75 (although one death notice, in the *Cambridge Independent Press* of 21 January 1865, gave his age as 70). The obituary noted that 'Mr Hooper had no family, but has left behind him a widow who knew his worth, and showed her devotion to him in sickness and in health, and has fully entitled herself to all the sympathy and condolence that could be shown her in her heavy and bitter bereavement'.

REFERENCES 121

17. David Garratt, 'The Theatre Royal, Oxford' (2011), www.arthurlloyd.co.uk/OxfordTheatres/TheatreRoyalOxford.htm
18. Obituary of Edward Hooper, *Oxford Times*, 14 January 1865
19. *The London Gazette*, Part 2 (1845)
20. *London Evening Standard*, 2 October 1845; Cheltenham Looker-on, 6 October 1838
21. *Oxford Chronicle and Reading Gazette*, 8 July 1865
22. *Oxford Times*, 5 August 1865
23. *Oxford Times*, 5 August 1865. George Maskell was found drowned in the river Clyde at Gourock, Scotland, in January 1881, a sad end for a popular comedian (*Dundee Advertiser*, 28 January 1881)
24. *Oxford Chronicle and Reading Gazette*, 7 October 1865
25. David Garratt, 'The Theatre Royal, Oxford' (2011), www.arthurlloyd.co.uk/OxfordTheatres/TheatreRoyalOxford.htm. The last press mention of Mrs Hooper at the Theatre Royal, Cambridge, was on 27 June 1868 (Cambridge Chronicle and Journal), when it was announced that Mr W. Sidney would be replacing her as in managing the theatre; I cannot find a definitive record of her after this.
26. *Oxford Chronicle and Reading Gazette*, 9 June 1866
27. *The Stage*, 8 September 1882
28. *Banbury Guardian*, 19 November 1896
29. *Banbury Guardian*, 10 January 1895
30. *Oxford Times*, 3 February 1900
31. *Oxford Times*, 24 March 1900; *Oxford Times*, 21 April 1900
32. *Oxford Times*, 10 February 1900
33. Oxford Times, 18 September 1909
34. *Oxford Times*, 21 December 1907
35. *Banbury Advertiser*, 6 August 1941
36. *Banbury Advertiser*, 5 December 1945
37. 'Oxford Playhouse – A Short History', www.oxfordplayhouse.com/about-us/oxford-playhouse-a-history/
38. At this time, the Berlin Quartet comprised Dr Joachim, Professor Kruse, Professor Wirth and Professor Hausmann (*Oxford Times*, 12 March 1898).

39. *Oxford Times*, 5 April 1890
40. *Oxford Chronicle and Reading Gazette*, 7 October 1865
41. *Oxford Times*, 5 March 1910
42. Mrs Edith Mary Lyttelton Gell (born 1861) was the wife of a rector's son, Philip, who gained both his BA and MA at Oxford (being a graduate of Balliol College). Philip Lyttelton Gell (born 1852) became a member of the Inner Temple in 1876, the year he gained his BA, but by 1891 was the manager of the Clarendon Press. Edith was formerly the Honourable Edith Mary Brodrick, daughter of Viscount William Middleton Brodrick and his wife, Lady Augusta Brodrick, née Fremantle. Edith Mary Brodrick married Philip in 1889, in Hambledon, Surrey. Both Mary and Philip had been born in London, and by 1911, they had moved back down there, where Philip described himself as of 'private means and director of public companies', as well as being Justice of the Peace. Mary's occupation was given as 'private means and literature', and 'Honourable' was added in the census margin, next to her name. The couple had no children. Edith Mary Gell died at Hopton Hall, in Wirksworth, Derbyshire, on 17 April 1944, aged 83 – 18 years after her husband's death.
43. *Oxford Times*, 10 February 1900
44. *Banbury Advertiser*, 10 November 1881
45. Patricia A. Cunningham, *Reforming Women's Fashion, 1850–1920: Politics, Health and Art* (Kent State University Press, Kent, Ohio, 2003), 50
46. *Reynolds's Newspaper*, 5 September 1858
47. *Dundee Courier*, 10 July 1866
48. *Reading Mercury*, 16 August 1851
49. *Oxford Chronicle and Reading Gazette*, 25 October 1851
50. *Oxford Journal*, 30 September 1899
51. *Western Morning News*, 6 September 1897
52. *Oxford University and City Herald*, 3 February 1866
53. *Oxford Chronicle and University Gazette*, 17 May 1856
54. *Oxford Times*, 3 October 1884
55. *Oxford Times*, 31 March 1877
56. *Oxford Times*, 15 April 1893

Chapter 7: Prison life

1. Richard Clark, 'Oxford Gaol – later HMP Oxford', http://www.capitalpunishmentuk.org/Oxford.pdf
2. *Banbury Advertiser*, 15 May 1856
3. *Oxford University and City Herald*, 1 March 1862
4. *Oxford University and City Herald*, 20 May 1854
5. Anon, *Regulations of the Oxford Female Penitentiary* (Oxford, 1834), 6
6. *Regulations of the Oxford Female Penitentiary*, 7
7. *Regulations of the Oxford Penitentiary*, 8
8. *Oxford University and City Herald*, 20 May 1854
9. *Oxford Times*, 21 June 1902
10. Stephanie Jenkins, 'Holywell Manor House', Oxford History (http://oxfordhistory.org.uk/holywell/misc/holywell_manor.html)
11. Susan Mumm, "Not Worse Than Other Girls': The Convent-Based Rehabilitation of Fallen Women in Victorian Britain', *Journal of Social History* (Spring 1996), 29:3, 527–547, accessed at http://oro.open.ac.uk/82/1/NOT_WORSE_THAN_OTHER_GIRLS.pdf.
12. *Regulations of the Oxford Penitentiary*, 11–12
13. *Oxford Times*, 21 June 1902
14. The Sisters of Mercy in charge of the Penitentiary in 1881 were older: Sister Superior Harriet Parish was 52, and the other sisters were aged between 31 and 76.
15. Richard Clark, 'Oxford Gaol – later HMP Oxford', www.capitalpunishmentuk.org/Oxford.pdf.
16. Using Richard Clark's list of executions from 1837 to 1964, at www.capitalpunishmentuk.org
17. *North Devon Journal*, 16 March 1876
18. 1881 census for HM Prison Oxford, St Thomas, Oxford
19. *Derby Daily Telegraph*, 4 November 1910
20. www.capitalpunishmentuk.org/Oxford.pdf
21. *Oxford Times*, 29 October 1864
22. *Oxford Journal*, 22 July 1882
23. *Oxford Journal*, 28 May 1892

24. Ibid
25. *Salisbury and Winchester Journal*, 15 July 1871; England & Wales, Criminal Registers, 1791–1892, on Ancestry. There is a record of the marriage of a Rachel Busby, aged 22, to shoemaker Albert Panant, on 21 March 1876 at St Barnabas in Oxford, which might be the same woman; she gives her address as 32 Wellington Street, and her father as stonemason Thomas Busby. This Rachel divorced her husband in 1887, citing his adultery and the fact that he had deserted her for the previous two years. By the time she made her divorce petition, she was working as a domestic servant in Streatham, south London.
26. *Northampton Mercury*, 8 July 1871
27. *Northampton Mercury*, 22 July 1871
28. *Northampton Mercury*, 8 July 1871
29. England & Wales, Criminal Registers, 1791–1892, on Ancestry
30. T. R. Malthus, *An Essay on the Principle of Population* (Oxford World's Classics, OUP, 2008), 13. Adverts for 'Malthusian appliances' were particularly common in the last decade of the nineteenth century and in the early years of the twentieth (see, for example, *Bradford Daily Telegraph*, 14 May 1896; *Illustrated Police News*, 9 March 1901).
31. Other family members might also be insured and then murdered for the policy payout – Margaret Higgins and Catherine Flannagan were hanged in 1884 after they murdered various individuals, including Catherine's son and Margaret's stepdaughter, for their insurance policies (see Richard Clark, 'Catherine Flannagan and Margaret Higgins – the 'Liverpool Borgias'', on CapitalPunishmentUK (www.capitalpunishmentuk.org/Flannagan_Higgins.html).
32. *Oxford Journal*, 28 May 1892
33. www.capitalpunishmentuk.org/Oxford.pdf
34. There is no death record for a female Kempson in the Oxford area for this time (which would be recorded in the July-September records), but this is because the death of Annie L. Kempson, 58, is actually recorded in the records for the October-December quarter of 1931. Annie Louisa Reynolds

married William John Kempson in Headington in 1905, and William J. Kempson died, aged 72, in 1925.
35. *Gloucester Citizen*, 4 August 1931
36. *Derby Daily Telegraph*, 5 August 1931
37. *Dundee Evening Telegraph*, 17 August 1931
38. *Hull Daily Mail*, 6 November 1931
39. *The Scotsman*, 24 November 1931; *The Scotsman*, 25 November 1931. The police were right in assuming that Annie's killer was a burglar; records suggest that Henry Daniel Seymour had a history of theft, including stealing £200-worth of jewellery from a man in Sevenoaks, Kent, in 1923. At the trial for that offence, at Kent Assizes, Seymour admitted previous convictions, and also asked the court to take into account a previous theft in Northampton, where he had stolen more than £5000 in cash. At that trial, he was convicted and sentenced to five years' penal servitude (The Scotsman, 19 February 1923).
40. *Aberdeen Press & Journal*, 28 November 1931; Larne Times, 19 December 1931

Chapter 8: Active citizens
1. 'The struggle for democracy: Trade unionism', The National Archives, http://www.nationalarchives.gov.uk/pathways/citizenship/struggle_democracy/trade_unionism.htm
2. *Oxford Times*, 12 February 1898
3. The references to Matilda, according to the conventions of the time, are to 'Mrs Henry Nettleship'; her first name therefore had to be checked on the 1891 census for 17 Bradmore Road, showing that Matilda Nettleship was born around 1843 in Harrow-on-the-Hill. Henry Nettleship died on 10 July 1893, and probate was granted to his widow; he had married the then Matilda Steel in Middlesex in 1870. She was the daughter of the master of Harrow School, and died in Petersfield, Hampshire, on 16 September 1920.
4. A report about the Oxford Prize Scheme for Needlework and Self-Help Association back in 1892 also recorded a Mrs Nettleship as being involved; although this is likely to have

been Matilda, her mother-in-law, who died in 1898, was still alive at this point, so there is a slight possibility it could have been her (*Oxford Journal*, 11 June 1892).
5. Charlotte Maria Toynbee (née Atwood), dealt with the accounts at Lady Margaret Hall, but was against women's suffrage, and in the 1890s, did not like the attempts being made to allow women to take Oxford's BA degree. However, she was a proponent of individual self-reliance, and Oxford's first female poor law guardian. As the latter, she argued for the abolition of outdoor relief and its replacement by pensions, in order to improve the 'independence' of the poor, and remove the sense of degradation she believed the respectable poor felt at receiving relief (Frances Lannon, 'Toynbee [nee Atwood], Charlotte Maria (1841–1931)', Oxford Dictionary of National Biography (2004)).
6. *Oxford Times*, 19 November 1892
7. *Oxford Journal*, 11 June 1887
8. Ibid
9. Elizabeth Crawford, *The Women's Suffrage Movement in Britain and Ireland*, 108. Crawford refers to the organisation as 'the Oxford Church of England's Women's Temperance Society'.
10. *Oxford Times*, 12 March 1910
11. Ibid
12. Ibid
13. Daniel Weinbren, 'The Fraternity of Female Friendly Societies' in Máire Fedelma Cross (ed), *Gender and Fraternal Orders in Europe, 1300-2000*, 209
14. *Reading Mercury*, 12 November 1892
15. Daniel Weinbren, 'Supporting Self-Help: Charity, Mutuality, and Reciprocity in Nineteenth-Century Britain', in Bernard Harris and Paul Bridgen (eds), *Charity and Mutual Aid in Europe and North America since 1800*, 75
16. Daniel Weinbren, 'The Fraternity of Female Friendly Societies', 210
17. *Reading Mercury*, 11 November 1893
18. It was also known as the Women's Protection and Provident Society, the Oxford Working Women's Protective and

Provident Society, and the Protection and Provident Society of Women Working in Trades in Oxford. In November 1886, the deputy mayor of Oxford had stated that the society had been in existence for 'some four or five years' (*Oxford Journal*, 20 November 1886); in February 1895, the society's thirteenth annual meeting was held (*Oxford Journal*, 9 February 1895).
19. As John B. Smethurst has stated, the society had a 'grandiose title' but was actually a 'tiny general organisation', relatively speaking; yet it was well thought of, and existed until 1913 (John B. Smethurst in Arthur Marsh and John B. Smethurst, *Historical Directory of Trade Unions, volume 5* (online, no page number given)).
20. *Oxford Journal, 20 November 1886*
21. Ibid
22. Ibid
23. Ann Tyrrell, 67, had died in the March quarter of 1891 in the Headington district; Rhoda Randall, 62, died in the June quarter of 1891, again in the Headington district.
24. *Oxford Journal*, 28 November 1891
25. J.C. Wilson was remembered, on his death in 1905, as having been very active within Oxford society, having been Chair of the Board of Guardians for many years, and a member of the School Board, as well as being the university's first alderman. (Exeter College Association, 'Register 2007', 62–63, https://staging.exeter.ox.ac.uk/wp-content/uploads/2017/07/register-07.pdf)
26. 1891 census for 98 Great Clarendon Street, Oxford.
27. *Oxford Journal*, 9 February 1895
28. *Oxford Journal*, 21 February 1891
29. The newspaper referred to Sarah simply as 'Mrs Woodward', but a check of the 1891 census shows that it was Sarah Woodward who was living at 236 Cowley Road, with her husband William and 33-year-old daughter Agatha.
30. *Oxford Journal*, 21 February 1891
31. For example, another branch was meeting in Bradford in November 1883 (*Leeds Mercury*, 15 November 1883), and in Bath in February of that year (*Bath Chronicle*, 1 February 1883).
32. *Oxford Times*, 10 November 1900

33. *Oxford Times*, 22 November 1902
34. Ibid
35. Ibid
36. 'Oxford Ladies' Association for the Care of Friendless Girls', Archive Catalogue, Oxfordshire History Centre.
37. *Oxford Times*, 22 November 1902
38. It is not clear whether the Mrs Liddell mentioned so frequently in press reports is Emma Liddell, or Lorina Liddell, the wife of Henry, dean of Christ Church, and mother of the better known Alice Liddell. Given that Lorina Liddell (1826–1910) was very active within Oxford society, she seems a more likely candidate.
39. Kelly's Directory for 1903, on Ancestry; *Bucks Advertiser and Free Press*, 13 June 1914
40. As is frustratingly often the case, in its report about this case, the newspapers merely referred to the women as 'Mrs' or 'Miss'. However, the mayor of Oxford at this time was city grocer James Hughes, and his wife was Jane.
41. Alexander William Hall (1838–1919), who was educated at Exeter College, was MP for Oxford 1874–80, 1881–85 and 1885–92. He and Emma married in 1863, when Emma was 19; she died, aged 85, in 1929.
42. *Oxford Journal*, 29 January 1887
43. *Oxford Times*, 5 March 1910. Miss Courtenay Bell was presumably Margaret Courtenay Bell, who died the following year, aged 50. Her younger brother Charles, with whom she lived, worked at the Ashmolean Museum. The only Mrs Kennett-Hayes I can locate in Oxford at this time would be Alice, 58, who lived at 5 Oriel Street; her husband Tom was a bookbinder. The Mrs Montagu Burrows mentioned here is likely to have been Isabella Christina Burrows, aged 47. She was married to Stephen Montagu Burrows, a retired civil servant and chairman of the Oxford Society for the Blind, and lived at 9 Norham Gardens (it could not have been Mary Anna, the wife of modern history professor Montagu Burrows, as she died in 1906, aged 89).

44. http://blogs.bodleian.ox.ac.uk/archivesandmanuscripts/tag/womens-unionist-organisation/ and 1911 census for Cranham Lodge, Reigate
45. http://spartacus-educational.com/Leducation70.htm
46. *Oxford Journal*, 2 March 1872
47. *Oxford Journal*, 16 December 1876; Simon Wenham, 'The Darker Side of the Oxford Suffragette Movement', http://simonwenham.com/arson-and-acid-the-darker-side-of-the-oxford-suffragette-movement/
48. Stephanie Jenkins, 'Oxford History: Oxford Mayors and Lord Mayors', www.oxfordhistory.org.uk/mayors/1836_1962/tawney_lily_1933.html and Lawrence Goldman, *The Life of RH Tawney: Socialism and History* (Bloomsbury Academic, 2014).
49. Supplement to the *London Gazette*, 2 January 1939, page 12
50. *Reynolds's Newspaper*, 4 December 1859
51. See, for example, *Oxford Times*, 27 October 1866; *Oxford Chronicle and Reading Gazette*, 6 October 1866.
52. *Banbury Advertiser*, 2 May 1872
53. *Salisbury Times*, 6 February 1875
54. *Oxford Times*, 13 April 1878; Elizabeth Crawford, *The Women's Suffrage Movement*, 51
55. Janet Horowitz Murray and Myra Stark (eds), *The Englishwoman's Review of Social and Industrial Questions, 1885* (Routledge, 1985), 115
56. John Simkin, 'Lilias Ashworth Hallett', Spartacus Educational (1997, revised 2015), http://spartacus-educational.com/WhallettA.htm
57. *Norwich Mercury*, 13 March 1880
58. *Oxford Times*, 17 December 1887
59. Ibid
60. *Oxford Journal*, 3 August 1889
61. *Oxford Journal*, 27 October 1888
62. *Oxfordshire Telegraph*, 1 August 1888. Flora's request for a cremation was covered by both the London and provincial press across Britain over a period of two weeks in August.

63. Press coverage of Flora Ritchie's cremation suggests that Miss Macdonald may have been sharing secretary duties with Flora before the latter's death, perhaps because of her illness, and so had become sole secretary afterwards.
64. *Oxford Journal*, 27 October 1888
65. Ibid
66. *Oxford Journal* 10 June 1899; Elizabeth Crawford, *The Women's Suffrage Movement*, 99
67. Simon Wenham, 'The Darker Side of the Oxford Suffragette Movement', http://simonwenham.com/arson-and-acid-the-darker-side-of-the-oxford-suffragette-movement/. Jessie was the daughter of Robert Payne Smith, Dean of Canterbury.
68. Elizabeth Crawford, *The Women's Suffrage Movement*, 109. No details of 'Miss Farnell' are given, but a Mrs Farnell – Elizabeth Radbone Farnell – was living in Oxford at this time; she was the wife of Christ Church College's manciple, John Jonathan Farnell, mother of several children, and fits the demographic of many of the suffrage supporters in Oxford. Mrs Haverfield could have been Winifred Ethel Haverfield, 30, the wife of Francis, a professor at Oxford University; she was also the daughter of a schools' inspector.
69. *Morning Post*, 18 October 1909
70. 'Mr Shackleton' was the Labour trade unionist MP David Shackleton (later Sir David), a 'champion of women's suffrage' (Blackburn with Darwen Council, 'Sir David Shackleton', Cotton Town, http://www.cottontown.org/Politics/Blackburn%20Members%20of%20Parliament/Pages/David-Shackleton.aspx).
71. *Oxford Times*, 25 June 1910
72. 'Suffragettes and Oxford High', http://oxfordhigh.gdst.net/ss-our-history-suffragettes/
73. *Oxford Times*, 9 July 1910
74. Simon Wenham, *The Darker Side of the Oxford Suffragette Movement*
75. Andrew Ffrench and Dan Robinson, 'Following the trail of the suffragettes', *Oxford Mail* (28 February 2014)

Primary Works Consulted

Websites
www.oxfordhistory.org.uk
www.headington.org.uk
www.southoxford.org./local-history-in-south-oxford/interesting-aspects-of-grandpont-and-south-oxford-s-history/the-coming-of-the-railway-to-oxford
www.ancestry.co.uk
www.findmypast.co.uk
www.thegenealogist.co.uk
www.britishnewspaperarchive.co.uk
www.bbc.co.uk/wales/history/sites/themes/society/women_teaching.shtml
http://oxfordhigh.gdst.net/senior-school/ss-about-us/
www.ox.ac.uk/about/oxford-people/women-at-oxford
www.st-annes.ox.ac.uk/about/history
www.freebmd.org.uk
www.twitter.com/lmhoxford
www.parksandgardens.org/places-and-people/person/1167
www.bodleian.ox.ac.uk/oua/enquiries/first-woman-graduate
http://global.oup.com/uk/archives/8.html#
www.workhouses.org.uk/
https://address-search.co.uk/business/20017278/New-Excelsior-Cafe-250-Cowley-Road-OXFORD-OX4-1UH/
https://web.archive.org/web/20131205044715/http://www.oxford-coveredmarket.co.uk:80/content/beginnings-1771
https://web.archive.org/web/20131205211905/http://www.oxford-coveredmarket.co.uk:80/content/other-business
www.bbc.co.uk/history/historic_figures/snow_john.shtml

www.oxfordshirehealtharchives.nhs.uk/tales-from-archive/cholera.htm
http://discovery.nationalarchives.gov.uk/details/c/F53065
www.nhs.uk/NHSEngland/thenhs/nhshistory/Pages/NHShistory1948.aspx
www.ouh.nhs.uk/hostpitals/jr/history.aspx
www.ashfordstpeters.nhs.uk/19th-century-mental-health
www.oxfordshirehealtharchives.nhs.uk/hospitals/littlemore_hospital.htm
www.boswells.co.uk/about-us
www.arthurlloyd.co.uk/OxfordTheatres/TheatreRoyalOxford.htm
www.oxfordplayhouse.com/about-us/oxford-playhouse-a-history
www.capitalpunishmentuk.org
www.nationalarchives.gov.uk/pathways/citizenship/struggle_democracy/trade_unionism.htm
https://staging.exeter.ox.ac.uk/wp-content/uploads/2017/07/register-07.pdf
http://oxfordhigh.gdst.net/ss-our-history-suffragettes/
http://blogs.bodleian.ox.ac.uk/archivesandmanuscripts/tag/womens-unionist-organisation/

Books

Acland, Henry Wentworth, *Memoir on the cholera at Oxford in the year 1854, with considerations suggested by the epidemic* (John Churchill, London, 1856)

Adams, Pauline, *Somerville for Women: An Oxford College 1879–1993* (Oxford University Press, 1996)

Brittain, Vera, *The Women at Oxford: A Fragment of History* (George G Harrap & Co, London, 1960)

Cox, Pamela and Annabel Hobley, *Shopgirls* (Hutchinson, 2014)

Crawford, Elizabeth, *The Women's Suffrage Movement in Britain and Ireland: A Regional Survey* (Routledge, Abingdon, 2006)

Cross, Máire Fedelma (ed.), *Gender and Fraternal Orders in Europe, 1300-2000* (Palgrave Macmillan, Basingstoke, 2010)

Crossley, Alan and C. R. Elrington (eds.), *A History of the County of Oxford: Volume 4, the City of Oxford* (VCH, London, 1979)

Cunningham, Patricia A., *Reforming Women's Fashion, 1850–1920: Politics, Health and Art* (Kent State University, Kent, Ohio, 2003)
Goldman, Lawrence, *The Life of RH Tawney: Socialism and History* (Bloomsbury Academic, 2014)
Harris, Bernard and Paul Bridgen (eds.), *Charity and Mutual Aid in Europe and North America since 1800* (Routledge, Abingdon, 2007)
Jenkins, Stanley C., *Oxford Suburbs and Villages Through Time: St Giles, Headington and St Clements, Cowley, Iffley, Wytham* (Amberley Publishing, Stroud, 2013)
Mander, W. J., *British Idealism: A History* (Oxford University Press, 2011)
Manley, Deborah, *Women in Oxford* (Heritage Tours Publications, Oxford, 1997)
Malthus, T. R., *An Essay on the Principle of Population* (Oxford University Press, 2008)
Marsh, Arthur and John B. Smethurst, *Historical Directory of Trade Unions, Volume 5* (Routledge, 2016)
Murray, Janet Horowitz and Myra Stark (eds.), *The Englishwoman's Review of Social and Industrial Questions, 1885* (Routledge, 1985)
Smith, Bonnie G., *Changing Lives: Women in European History since 1700* (DC Heath & Co, 1989)

Theses
Graham, Malcolm, *The Suburbs of Victorian Oxford: Growth in a Pre-Industrial City* (PhD thesis, University of Leicester, 1985)

Articles
Abellán, Javier, 'Water supply and sanitation services in modern Europe: developments in 19th-20th centuries' (2017), 12th International Conference of Economic History, University of Salamanca
Anon, 'Regulations of the Oxford Female Penitentiary' (Oxford, 1834)
Boughton, John, 'The Blackbird Leys Estate, Oxford: 'Never accepted as part of the city proper" (2013), https://

municipaldreams.wordpress.com/2013/05/07/the-blackbird-leys-estate-oxford-never-part-of-the-city-proper/

Brown, Derek, '1945–51: Labour and the creation of the welfare state', *The Guardian*, 14 March 2001, www.theguardian.com/politics/2001/mar/14/past.education

Clark, Richard, 'Catherine Flannagan and Margaret Higgins – the 'Liverpool Borgias'', www.capitalpunishmentuk.org/Flannagan_Higgins.html

Clark, Richard, 'Oxford Gaol – later HMP Oxford', www.capitalpunishmentuk.org/Oxford.pdf

French, Andrew and Dan Robinson, 'Following the trail of the suffragettes', *Oxford Mail*, 28 February 2014, www.oxfordmail.co.uk/news/11043179.Following_the_trail_of_the_suffragattes/

Hannabuss, Keith, 'Eleanor Elizabeth Smith (1822–1896)', *Oxford Dictionary of National Biography*

Hannabuss, Keith, 'Smith, Henry John Stephen (1826–1883)', *Oxford Dictionary of National Biography*

Hassall, T.G., 'Excavations at 44–46 Cornmarket Street, Oxford, 1970', *Oxoniensia* (1971), pp.15–36

Howarth, Janet, 'Sidgwick, Arthur (1840–1920)', *Oxford Dictionary of National Biography*

Lannon, Frances, 'Toynbee [nee Atwood], Charlotte Maria (1841–1931)', *Oxford Dictionary of National Biography*

Moss, Andrew, 'The RI: A Medical History', *Oxford Today* (Trinity issue, 2007)

Mumm, Susan, ''Not worse than other girls': the convent-based rehabilitation of fallen women in Victorian Britain', *Journal of Social History* (Spring 1996), 29:3, pp.527–547

Neeleman, J., 'Suicide as a crime in the UK: legal history, international comparisons and present implications', *Acta Psychiatrica Scandinavica*, 94:4 (1996), pp.252–257

Simkin, John, 'Lilias Ashworth Hallett', Spartacus Educational (1997, revised 2015), http://spartacus-educational.com/WhallettA.htm

Simon Wenham, 'The Darker Side of the Oxford Suffragette Movement', http://simonwenham.com/arson-and-acid-the-darker-side-of-the-oxford-suffragette-movement/

Chapters in edited books

Weinbren, Daniel, 'The Fraternity of Female Friendly Societies' in Cross (ed), *Gender and Fraternal Orders in Europe, 1300–2000* (as before)

Weinbren, Daniel, 'Supporting Self-Help: Charity, Mutuality and Reciprocity in Nineteenth-Century Britain', in Harris and Bridgen (eds.), *Charity and Mutual Aid in Europe and North America since 1800* (as before)

Index

Air Raid Precautions (ARP), 42
Asquith, Herbert, 91

Bevan, Aneurin (Nye), 54
Beveridge Report, 54
Birth control, 56
    see also sex
    see also marriage
Bloomerism, also Bloomers, 69–72
    see also National Dress Reform
        Association, 69–70
Board of Guardians, 96, 100, 127
British Red Cross, 56
Businesses;
    Boswell's, 62–3, 120, 132
    City Drapery Stores, 18
    F. Cape & Co, 18–20, 46, 71, 107
    Cooper's Jam, 47, 116
    Educational Supply Store, 63
    Fridette's French Hat Shop, 62
    May's Drug Company, 62
    Oxford Drug Company,
        62–3, 120
    Oxford University Press, 22, 34,
        45, 68
    Samuel Evans' drapery, 19
    Joseph King's bakery, 19
    Marks & Spencer, 20
    NAAFI, 21

Cafés;
    Cadena Café, 20, 46, 116
    Café no 3, 42

Lloyd's Oriental Café, 46
Oxford Café and Dining Rooms,
    44–5
Railway Café, 44
Victoria Coffee House, 43
see also Temperance
Central Midwives Board, 57
Childcare, 16, 25, 32, 34, 55
    see also governesses
    see also servants
Church, 37, 77, 86, 88
Churches;
    Christ Church, 9, 101, 128
    St Clements, 84
    St Cross, 76
    St Giles, 7, 10
    St Margaret, 32
    St Mary the Virgin, 35, 90
Colleges;
    Balliol, 104, 122
    Brasenose, 26
    Christ Church, 42, 130
    Corpus Christi, 4–5, 87
    Hertford, 89, 115
    Jesus, 84, 104
    Keble, 37, 115
    Lady Margaret Hall, 5, 7–8, 21,
        105, 111, 126
    Lincoln, 5
    Magdalen, 10, 30, 54, 107
    Merton, 5, 100
    Oriel, 12, 52
    Pembroke, 30, 54

St Anne's, 5
St Hilda's, 6–7
St Hugh's, 6, 10, 112
St John's, 68, 107
Somerville, 5–6, 8–9,
   12–13, 21, 111
Trinity, 93
University College, 5, 11, 111
Worcester College, 9
Combinations;
   see Trade Unions
Convent;
   see Sisters of Mercy
Council housing, 29, 31
Cremation, 104, 129, 130
   Cremation Society of
      England, 104
Cricket;
   see Victoria Cricket Club 43
Crime;
   assault, 74, 81–2
      see also domestic violence
   Assizes, Oxford, 80, 83
   Bloody Code, 79
   capital offences, 79, 83
   concealment of birth, 80, 83
   domestic violence, 81
   hangings, 79
   infanticide, 80, 83
      see also concealment of birth
   murder, 79–81, 83–5, 124
   petty sessions, 56, 74
   petty treason, 79
   poison, 59
   police court, 35, 81
   prison, 53, 74, 78–80, 82,
      84–5, 123
   theft, 74, 85, 125
   warders, prison, 80, 85
   see also suicide
   see also Penitentiary,
      Female
Croydon, Bishop of, 89

Death;
   Childbed, in, 60
   Disease, 53
   Drink, 90
   Financial impact, x, 32
   Infant and childhood
      deaths, 57, 60
   Poverty and, 53, 60
   Premature, 6, 104
   Universality of experience, 39
   Death rates, 53
   see also cremation
   see also crime
   see also suicide
Defence of the Realm Act, 91
Disease;
   Cholera, 52–3, 56, 117, 132
   Choleraic diarrhoea, 52
   Venereal disease, 55
Divorce, 33–6, 81, 89,
   114, 124
Divorce Court, 33, 89
   see also Divorce

Education;
   Association for Promoting the
      Higher Education of Women
      (AEW), 5, 8–9, 12
   Cheltenham Ladies'
      College, 6
   Christ Church Cathedral
      School, 9
   governesses, 1, 3, 14, 16, 22,
      23–4, 26
   legislation;
      Elementary Education Act
         1870, 1, 100
      Elementary Education Act
         1880, 1
   local education
      authorities, 1
   local examinations, 4,
      9–10, 23

Oxford High School for Girls, 2, 35, 68, 106
school boards, 1, 100, 127
Society of Home-Students, 5, 7, 112
see also colleges

Families;
  class of, 98
  divorce,
    see marriage
  Friendly Societies and, 92
  lodgers, taking in, 5
  male members, x
  money and, x, 28, 37, 39, 84, 108
  orphans, 38, 54, 98
  servants, 22, 32
  spinsters, 2, 32, 36
  stepmothers, 34
  values, 36
  war, 37
  wives, 47
  women's work within, 28, 49, 50, 108
  workhouse, 31

Hope Cottage, 78
House of Refuge;
  see Penitentiary, Female
Hospitals;
  maternity home, 57
  Radcliffe Infirmary, 56–7
  school of nursing, 56
  see also Central Midwives Board
Hotels;
  Clarendon Hotel, 28, 42
  Dodson's Temperance Hotel, 41–2
  Randolph Hotel, 40–1

Illegitimacy, 56, 80, 83, 108

Judges' Lodgings, 2

Lodgings, 19, 21, 27, 40, 44, 59, 64, 108

Maintenance, 34, 97
Marriage;
  abandonment, 34, 36
  adultery, 33, 35–6, 124
  advertisements, 32
  affairs, 33–6, 56
  children, 37
  cruelty, 36
  divorce, 33–6, 81, 89, 114, 124
  engagements, 32
  gossip, 81
  maintenance, 34
  neglect, 33
  respectability, 32
  separation, 34, 36, 81
  sex, 36–7, 56, 97
Matrimonial Causes Act, 33, 36
Mental health, 31, 109, 132
  asylums,
    see workhouse
  delusions, 59
  depression, 58–59, 60, 83
  idiots,
    see lunatics
  imbeciles,
    see lunatics
  lunatics, 58
  Lunacy Act, 57
  nervous breakdown, 59
  schizophrenia, 58
  suicide, 59–60, 75, 119, 134
  see also workhouse
Music, 2, 23–4, 26, 33, 36, 46, 63, 68, 97, 100
  Oxford University Musical Club, 68

National Health Service, 32, 54, 118–19
Neglect (non-marital), 54, 82, 90

INDEX 139

Occupations;
   baker, 26, 48
   beer seller/retailer, 27,
     43, 48–9
   bookkeeper, 28
   chambermaid, 40–2
   confectioner, 27, 48
   dressmaker, 16–17, 27,
     55, 58, 102
   governesses,
     see education
   housekeeper, 12, 14, 28,
     36, 46, 52
   ironmonger, 26
   linen keeper, 41
   machinist, 28, 58
   milliner, 16, 62
   music seller, 26
   pastry cook, 27
   printer, 26
   secretary/typist, 24, 28
   servant, 16, 25–6, 31–2, 40
   shopgirl, 16, 18–20,
     112–13, 132
   shop-keeper, 20, 49–50, 101
   stationer, 26, 33, 43–4, 104
   teacher, 2, 18, 24, 32, 34, 43,
     46–7, 67, 97, 108
   wardrobe dealer, 27
Oxford;
   Bishop of, 71, 92
   Covered Market, 47, 117, 141
   Liberal Hall, 103
   Masonic Buildings, 99
   Norham Gardens, 98, 118, 138
   Oxford Local Board of Health,
     52, 65
   Oxford City Council, 30
   Oxford Town Hall, 3, 65–6, 68,
     99, 102, 105
   The Jam Factory, 47
   Wesleyan Lecture Room, 87,
     94–5

Organisations;
   British Federation of Social
     Workers, 37
   Church Society for Training the
     Speaking Voice, 69
   Girls' Friendly Society, 98
   Liberal Unionists, 68
   National Dress Reform
     Association, 69–70
   Oxford Charity Organisation
     Society (COS), 92
   Oxford Debating
     Society, 101
   Oxford Ladies'
     Association, 78
   Oxford Ladies' Association for
     the Care of Friendless Girls
     (LACFG), 96–7
   Oxford Reform Club, 103
   Oxford Society of Women
     Working in Trades, 87
   Oxford Women's Liberal
     Association, 103
   Oxford Working Women's
     Benefit Society, 92, 95–6
   Primrose League, 68
   Public Assistance
     Committee, 100
   Sick Benefit Society, 99
   Women's Help Society, 92
   Women's Home Missions
     Association, 98
   Women's Liberal Government
     Society, 105
   Women's National Advisory
     Committee, 100
   Women's Public Health Officers'
     Association, 37
   Women's Trade
     Society, 87, 99
   Women's Union, 89
   see also Cremation Society of
     England

see also suffrage movement
see also temperance

Pankhurst, Emmeline, 101
Pankhurst, Sylvia, 107
Penitentiary, Female, 75–9, 98, 123, 133
  see also crime
People's Tax, 91
Poor Law Amendment Act, 29, 54
Poor Law Unions, 29–30, 54
Poverty, 31, 53, 60, 82, 84, 89, 97
Prison;
  see crime
Prostitution, 53, 75–6, 82
Public houses (pubs), 42–3, 49, 88, 91, 107
  see also People's Tax

Railways, viii, 53, 110, 117
Rationing, 49–51, 109
Refugees, 14, 57
Religion, 77, 88, 103
  see also Churches
  see also Oxford, Bishop of

St Frideswide's Cottage, 79, 97
St Hilda's Hall;
  see colleges
St John the Baptist, Community of;
  see Sisters of Mercy
Sanitation, 52, 119, 133
Separation;
  see marriage
Servant registries, 25, 96
Sewage, 53, 55
Sex, 36–7, 56, 97
  see also marriage
  see also birth control

Shopping, 20, 61–3, 69, 85
Oxford Shopping Carnival, 63, 120
  see also businesses
  see also shopgirls
Sisters of Mercy, 76, 123
Suffrage movement;
  1911 census, 9
  Anti-Women's Suffrage Movement, 116
  House of Commons, 103, 116
  London Society for Women's Suffrage, 103
  Manchester Women's Suffrage Committee, 102
  Municipal Franchise Act, 101
  National Society for Women's Suffrage, 102
  National Union of Women's Suffrage Societies (NUWSS), 101, 105–106
  Oxford Women's Suffrage Society, 105–106
  Parliament (Qualification of Women) Act, 107
  Representation of the People Act, 107
  Sex Disqualification (Removal) Act, 1919, 2, 12
  Suffrage Society, 102
  Votes for Women Bill, 106
  Women's Social and Political Union (WSPU), 101
  see also Oxford Women's Liberal Association
  see also Pankhurst, Emmeline
  see also Pankhurst, Sylvia

Temperance;
  British Women's Temperance Association, 88

Church of England Temperance
    Society, 89, 126
Church of England Temperance
    Society's Women's
    Union, 89
Dodson's Temperance Hotel,
    41–2
  cafés and hotels, 41–2, 44,
    108–109
  intemperance and, 90
  meetings, 90–1
  societies, 86, 88, 90
  movement, 42, 88, 90–1
Theatres and theatre-going,
    63–8
  East Oxford Theatre, 67
  Lyric Hall, *also* Constitutional
    Hall, Empire Theatre of
    Varieties, 64, 67
  New Theatre, 62–4, 66
  Oxford Playhouse, 67,
    121, 132
  Oxford University Dramatic
    Society (OUDS), 63
  Star Assembly Room, 64
  Theatre Royal, 64, 66,
    68, 121
Tourism, viii–ix, 97
Trade Unions;
  Combination Acts, 86
  Oxford Society of Women
    Working in Trades, 87, 92, 127
  London Women's Trade
    Union League, 87
  Women's Protective and
    Provident Society,
    see Oxford Society of Women
    Working in Trades

University, 39, 68, 104
  admission of women, 4, 11–13,
    21–2, 109
  chaperones, 9, 11
  Congregation, 11
  cost, 5
  Debating Rooms, 103
  degrees, 6, 8–9, 11–13, 23, 69,
    108–109
  education, viii
  examinations, 8–10, 105
  formality of, 1
  Hebdomadal Council, 13
  history, ix
  lectures and lecturing,
    5, 9, 14
  lodgings, 27, 40
  male representatives, 3, 5,
    94, 98, 103
  Oxford Union, 13
  Oxford University
    Congregation, 11
  population, x, 3
  servants, 25
  students, x, 42
  terms, 63–4
  wartime, 12, 109
  see also colleges
  see also education
  see also Oxford University
    Musical Club

Victoria Cricket Club, 43

War;
  First World War;
    End of, 17
    Impact of, 26, 32, 45,
      49, 97
    Hospitals, 30, 55
    Outbreak of, 12, 20,
      91, 96
    Post-war period, 29, 100
  Second World War;
    Dig For Victory, 50
    Hospitals, 30, 55
    Impact of, 37, 49

Outbreak of, 20
Post-war, 31, 79
Theatre, 67
see also Rationing
Workhouses, x
    Board meetings, 96
    Conditions, 59
    Destitution, 32, 54

Establishment of, 29–30, 54
Higginbotham, Peter, 114, 118, 131
Inmates, 30–1, 55, 82
Mental health, 57
Requisitioning, 30